...shed as a lavishly illustrated hardback, this new paperback edition has double the number of new contributions from many well-known figures. The sale of every copy will support the campaigning work of CPRE, the organization which is dedicated to a beautiful and living countryside.

ICONS OF ENGLAND

Edited by

Bill Bryson

Campaign to Protect
Rural England

BLACK SWAN

TRANSWORLD PUBLISHERS
61–63 Uxbridge Road, London, W5 5SA
A Random House Group Company
www.rbooks.co.uk

ICONS OF ENGLAND
A BLACK SWAN BOOK: 9780552776356

First published in Great Britain
in 2008 by Think Books
Black Swan edition published 2010

Mixed Sources
Product group from well-managed
forests and other controlled sources
www.fsc.org Cert no. TT-COC-2139
© 1996 Forest Stewardship Council
FSC

THE CAMPAIGN TO PROTECT RURAL ENGLAND
warmly thanks all those who have contributed to this
book. We dedicate it to the many thousands of volunteers
who have worked so hard and given so freely of their
time since we were founded in 1926.

Campaign to Protect
Rural England

Registered charity no: 1089685
www.cpre.org.uk

CONTENTS

FOREWORD

His Royal Highness
The Prince of Wales

CLARENCE HOUSE

There is perhaps a rich irony in the fact that it takes an American, albeit one who has lived in these islands for many years, to recognize, celebrate and fight to preserve so much of what is precious about our country. There can be no-one who more deserves the title of "honorary Englishman" than Bill Bryson. Through his books, films and his campaigning as President of the Campaign to Protect Rural England he has done so much to help us appreciate the wonders and charms which surround us and to which, too often, we seem utterly blind. We all owe him the greatest possible debt, and so I could not be more pleased to write a foreword to this remarkable book, *Icons of England*.

And what greater icon could we have than our countryside, which I have always believed helps to define our identity as a nation? England is blessed with some of the most beautiful scenery in the world. The patchwork quilt of fields, moors, forests, villages, and market towns which spreads across this land is the product of a golden combination of Nature's gift to us and the toil and care of generations of farmers and their families who have managed the land. To me, it embodies England's very soul and is as precious as any Cathedral. The dry stone walls, the hedges, the thatched cottages, the village Churches, pubs, post offices and shops are at the heart of what it means to be English, as are the people whose skills and craftsmanship and commitment keep them alive.

For more than eighty years, the Campaign to Protect Rural England has been leading the fight to preserve the remaining delicate fabric of our countryside. The foresight of the founding fathers was extraordinary – in 1926 Clough Williams-Ellis, whom I remember well and admire greatly, published *England and the Octopus*, an anti-sprawl polemic, and in the same year Sir Patrick Abercrombie wrote his paper, *The Preservation of Rural England*. The fight has continued since then and great successes have been won. Indeed, the recent creation of the South Downs National Park, sixty years after it was first proposed, shows the importance of perseverance and is a huge cause for optimism. When we do all come together to work towards a goal, so much can be achieved. It gives me hope that we will not allow our traditions and heritage to be swept away, and that we will look once more to the land for nourishment, healing, wisdom and inspiration.

When asked what, for them, encapsulates the English countryside, the contributors to this book came up with a wide variety of personal icons, from a favourite landscape to a treasured monument, from a particular species of wildlife to a familiar rustic emblem or rural tradition. Together they have created an eclectic and richly varied celebration of England's countryside. I pray that this book will inspire us all to work tirelessly to preserve everything that is best in our magnificent countryside and to ensure that it remains at the very heart of our great island story.

INTRODUCTION

Bill Bryson
President, CPRE

YEARS AGO, WHEN I was brand new to Britain and everything was still a mystery to me, I went with an English friend to Brighton for the day, and there I saw my first seaside pier. The idea of constructing a runway to nowhere was one that would never have occurred to me. I asked her what it was for.

'Well, they let you walk out and see the sea,' she explained as if I were a little simple.

'But we can see the sea from here,' I pointed out.

'No, you don't understand. You walk out to the end and you are over the sea. It's lovely.'

'Can you see coral reefs and shipwrecks and things?' I asked hopefully.

'No, it's just murky water.'

'Can you see France?'

'Of course not. You just see the sea.' Her tone betrayed perhaps just a hint of exasperation. 'You take the air. It's very bracing.'

'And then what?'

'Then you walk back and have some whelks and stroll along the promenade and maybe ride a donkey on the beach – no, I don't know why; it's just something else we do – and then you have an ice cream and get on the train and go home.'

'And this is a fabulous day out?'

'Oh yes, it's lovely. Especially if it doesn't rain.'

I have since come to realize that she was right about everything but the whelks. (If you are reading this in another country and aren't familiar with that marine delicacy, you may get the same experience by finding an old golf ball, removing the cover and eating what remains. The only difference is that the golf ball has a little more flavour.) Indeed, after some thirty years of devoted observation, I have come to appreciate that the things that make England what it is – which is to say, like nowhere else on Earth – and however peculiar they may seem at first blush, are actually quite endearing and often deeply admirable. This is a book about those things.

Four qualities in particular, I think, set English icons apart and make them more memorable, more individual, vastly more noteworthy than icons elsewhere. Foremost among these is the ability – so gloriously evinced in the seaside pier – to be magnificent while having no evident purpose at all.

Consider one of my own favourite national glories, the wondrously artificial, profoundly inexplicable Silbury Hill in Wiltshire – the largest man-made mound in Europe. Built at about the same time as Stonehenge, it covers five acres and rises 130 feet above the surrounding landscape. It is positively immense, and involved an almost unimaginable commitment of labour. Yet Silbury Hill has no known purpose. It is not a burial chamber and holds no treasures. It consists of nothing but soil and rock carefully formed into a large pudding-shaped hill. All that can be said for certain is that some people at some time in the very distant past decided, for purposes we cannot guess, to make a large hill where previously there had been none.

There really is a kind of national instinct for putting up interesting things whether there is a need for them or not. You see it in chalk horses carved in hillsides and Scottish brochs and drystone walls climbing up and over preposterously steep and craggy slopes. (Who cares where the sheep go when they get up there?) I have always been convinced that the starting point for Stonehenge was some guy standing on Salisbury Plain and saying: 'You know, what this place needs is some really big rocks.'

Which brings us to the second distinctive quality of English icons – their ubiquity. Let us rush to London, to modern times, so I can show you what I mean. We are at Hyde Park Corner roundabout, surrounded by a ceaseless flow of vehicles, gazing up at the enormous arched monument that stands on the parklike green island in its centre. Atop the monument is a large statue of a winged goddess on a chariot. The island is a surprisingly tranquil place, and in fact rather a lonely one, for few visitors find their way through the pedestrian tunnels that lead to it. Fewer still are aware that the arch contains a charming museum and a lift that takes you to a lookout terrace where you get one of the most splendid views in London. It is only way up here that you realize just what a large structure this is – and how startlingly outsized the statue on the roof is. It is the largest bronze sculpture in Europe. Only when you are up there does the scale of all this come into sudden focus. This is a monumental edifice indeed.

Now here is the really interesting thing about it. Ask anyone in London – any cab driver, any policeman, any citizen you care to collar – what the name of this arch is and hardly any of them can tell you. Although it is one of the most visible and driven-past monuments in London, on as prime a site as the city offers, it is utterly and enchantingly lost to consideration because it is just of one of hundreds and hundreds of historic, appreciable, glorious, iconic structures that exist in London. Almost anywhere else in the world this would be a celebrated monument. Here it is backdrop.

Part of the reason its name is not better known is that it has had several in the 180 years since it was built by the great Decimus Burton. At various times it has been known as Constitution Arch, Wellington Arch, Green Park Arch and now Wellington Arch again. You won't be surprised to hear that it is also quite useless and always has been. It was designed originally as an outer entryway to Buckingham Palace, but was such an impediment to traffic, and so completely out of scale, that it was moved to the traffic island in 1882 just to get it out of the way.

It is your good fortune in this country to have so many iconic treasures, but it is a danger too. Having so many means that they are easily forgotten and even lost – which is the third and most tragic of the qualities that set English icons apart. In the thirty years I have known England, you have lost, or all but lost, an appreciable number of iconic features – milk bottles, corner shops, village post offices, red phone boxes, seaside holidays and even some seaside piers, including the one at Brighton that so bemused and transfixed me thirty years ago.

Happily, there is a fourth and more encouraging quality to icons, as this book so engagingly attests: people love them. They don't just appreciate them, the way you might appreciate a good book or an expensive dinner. They love them like a child. National icons really are the things that set countries apart and yet they are almost always taken completely for granted, which means they often aren't missed until they are gone for good. So it is wonderful to see them given the warmth and reverence they deserve in the pages that follow.

This book is also a timely reminder of how lucky we are to have a heroic outfit like the Campaign to Protect Rural England, to make sure that other iconic features – like Green Belts and hedgerows, long views over dreamy landscapes and a thousand things more – aren't lost as well.

Our job is to make sure that a book like this is always a celebration and not a memorial. These are thought-provoking and refreshing contributions. Many are anecdotes and memories that celebrate being in and enjoying the countryside as much as they praise historic monuments and locations. We are immensely grateful to all the writers who have contributed, including all those who wrote pieces for this new edition. We were especially pleased to receive a thoughtful and touching contribution from the great and kindly Miles Kington shortly before his tragically early death. And I enjoyed reading Mary Smith's 'Forever Tranquil', winner of the *Daily Telegraph* competition to write an entry for inclusion in this book. As for the rest of you, we can't thank you enough for your support.

IN SEARCH OF ENGLAND'S GNOMES

Kate Adie
on deer parks

I USED TO WONDER if deer were posh people's ornaments; the aristocratic equivalent of the garden gnome. For these animals do not seem real. They are never out of place in fairy tales, myths and legends – the stories of Herne the Hunter and Robin Hood. And although our history books seem full of them – the royals grew forests to hunt them in, Georgian landowners created parks to show them off, and the poor used to enjoy feasting on them – many people have never seen one. But if you are lucky enough – as I was in my childhood – to catch these enigmatic beings on show, you'll soon realize the countryside isn't quite the same without them.

As a child, it was a treat to take a run in the car into Swaledale or Teesdale, away from the industrial cranes and pitheads of the County Durham coast. On the way back, full of egg and tomato sandwiches and home-made shortbread, we would always stop on the edge of the village of Staindrop. Once there, I'd peer over the drystone wall towards the outline of Raby Castle and stare at its vast park of rather lumpy northern grassland, with a small copse here and there.

With luck came the moment when I could squeak, 'There they are!' as a clutch of brown thin-legged creatures would move tentatively into view – as if they'd been wondering whether it was worth putting themselves on show. Some would browse, others would stare snootily, and the antlered boss would stand at a distance, as king of the park. They would always adopt a rather grand pose, which I found amusing when accompanied by their silly twitching tails.

Up close, deer are delightful, if a bit dim. They're not interested in being pets; they have no desire to please; they won't come when they're called and go bananas when a sheepdog appears. They seem made to decorate the countryside – when they feel like it – and they're rather good at it. Not only are they elegant, but they always come as something of a surprise. Unlike cattle and sheep, which can be relied upon to be more or less where you expect to find them, deer play hide and seek. On rural roads, there are signs saying 'Caution: Deer'. You proceed cautiously, expecting a stag to leap up to your bonnet, or plant itself foursquare and elk-like in the middle of the tarmac. But they somehow never appear. They remain concealed in the greenery, and wait until you have passed, before strolling out, probably congratulating each other on maintaining the view in the village pub that 'they may or may not exist'.

For many people, a deer will never be anything more than an image of Bambi in a picture book. But it is worth making an effort to catch sight of the real thing. While elusive, they come into their own on country estates, when they eventually deign to graze in the sunshine. They stroll delicately, eyeing the landscape as they go – ready to bound into cover at the slightest hint of danger. Just watching them lets you imagine what it would be like to have been a poacher in the Middle Ages, longing for a portion of tender meat to supplement a dull diet, or a newly fortunate landowner dreaming of a landscaped park filled with handsome fallow and roe. For me as a child, the surprise of seeing deer was the icing on the cake, the unexpected bonus of a trip to the countryside. And waiting for them to appear was all part of the fun.

A PLACE IN THE COUNTRY

George Alagiah
on the English countryside

'MY PARENTS LIVE IN the country. Would you like to come and stay with us?' I can't remember if those were the exact words, but I do recall the fact that it was the first time I'd heard of 'the country'. This was 1967. I was eleven going on twelve, and had just arrived in England. I had moved from one country, Ghana, to this one, so I was confused: to what was my new English friend referring? Just weeks into what would become a lifetime attachment to England, I had already learned the most important lesson for an immigrant – don't embarrass yourself, just pretend you know what the locals are talking about. I accepted the offer and, some days later, found myself on the train from Portsmouth to Sussex.

I didn't fully understand it at the time. But on that little weekend retreat from our city school I encountered the country – not as a place, but as an idea. Back in Ghana, or further back still in Sri Lanka, where I was born, the ties with the rural areas were visceral. The countryside was what defined a person, the town or city merely the place where one made a living. Over the decades, with a second or even third generation born in the heat and dust of the towns, the enduring strength of the extended family pulls one back to the source of the bloodline – to the village or hamlet where it all began.

Here it is different. Here the power of the Industrial Revolution tipped the balance in favour of England's towns and cities. The smokestacks and tenements changed the physical landscape, but they also altered the mental landscape. The 'country' had to be reinvented as an escape and a refuge from the demands of urban living. Sometimes the countryside has been reduced to a leisure activity, a package deal shorn of nature's life-affirming rhythm, and cleansed of the muck and smell that is so much a part of rural life. But the real thing is there all the same – every right of way is an invitation, every stile a step into somewhere gentle and generous.

I write this after a long weekend in the fields and folds of North Cornwall and Devon. In one day we walked along the bank of the river Ottery, courtesy of an obliging farmer, tucked into some of the best pub grub in Lydford village and ended the afternoon underneath Widgery Cross on Brat Tor. From the granite mass that is Dartmoor, we watched a sinking sun's fading light settle on Cornwall, stretched out to the west like England's foot. To go from the verdant squelchy-welly track down to the Ottery's floodplain and then to the bleak and barren heights of Dartmoor is to experience, in the space of just a few hours, the infinite variety of this small island of ours.

The country is not so much another place as another state of mind. There is a trick to it, though. You have to leave the call of the BlackBerry behind. You need to stop when you feel like stopping, look when you feel like looking and talk when you feel like talking. And then you might learn, as we did from a local, that the reason hundreds of starlings in flight will twist and turn in unison is because the ones on the outside are constantly trying to get to the inside where they feel safer.

Some forty years on from that first trip, I finally understand what going to the country is all about. And now it's my turn to offer an invitation: 'Fancy a weekend in the country?'

FROM PILLAR TO POST

Peter Ashley

on postboxes

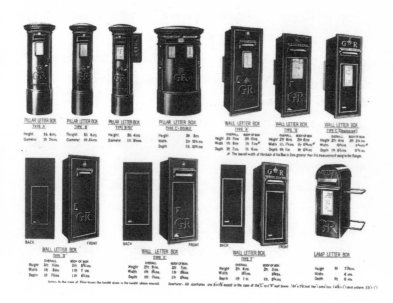

THE FIRST PILLAR BOX I saw was at the end of our road. It had a cream oval on the top with the words 'Post Office' and a red arrow pointing to the shop door two yards away. My mother would lift me up to it in order to send letters skimming into the darkness, and I remember being there when the postman unlocked its door with a key from a huge jangling bunch and started shovelling the mail into a rust-coloured sack.

I knew from comics that burglars used sacks, and had to be dissuaded by my mother from the notion that a theft was being committed. I had imagined that mail was collected in an underground cavern where tiny post elves – such as those in a Rupert Bear story – sorted it all out. The criminal element persisted when my brother told me that *when* (not *if*) I ended up in jail, all I could expect to be doing in my dungeon would be sewing mailbags.

Anthony Trollope is credited with introducing post-boxes to the Channel Islands in 1852, before knocking out his 'Barsetshire' novels. The boxes arrived on the mainland a year later in Botchergate, Carlisle. It is odd that the experiment didn't start in the capital – usually the test bed for innovation. The first pillar box in our present monarch's reign was planted near the Horse Guards in 1952.

The royal connection took on new relevance when I bought the little I-Spy book *In the Street*, and postboxes became quarries in a hunting game to spot royal ciphers. These cast-iron monograms enabled a rough chronology to be applied: the flowing script for Victoria, the spare initials for George V. Even Edward VIII found his cipher cast on to a few boxes before he decided to throw in the crown. Much later, I took pleasure in discovering the many variants of design. The early vertical-slitted box near Bishop's Caundle in Dorset; the acanthus leaves topping a Penfold hexagonal box in Chiswick; double boxes on city streets; airmail boxes in sky blue. And pillar boxes are not solely free-standing. Rural areas were served by boxes set into brick or stone walls; hump-backed and round-topped boxes clamped to tarred telegraph poles.

Icons of the English scene, pillar boxes stand like red and black guardsmen awaiting their orders. The perfect visual shorthand for communication, our digitalized cyberworld gives us nothing as potently recognizable. Remarkably, most of them are still with us, often all that stands between us and our messages, invitations, greetings and condolences reappearing – as if by magic – just about anywhere in the world. Occasionally they will be struck off the postman's rota. But they still obstinately cling on to pavements, grass verges and walls. They are difficult to uproot; like icebergs, there's almost as much below the pavement. One wall box – that once served Waddon Manor and other less grand abodes below Corton Down in Dorset – still revealed its fretwork grille sitting in the bottom when I cautiously opened the now unlocked heavy door. Apparently this is a snail trap, designed to prevent the shell-backed creatures from consuming the mail – how, I'm not quite sure.

I've always feared that these essential items in the iconography of England may one day disappear, or that in the spirit of the age I might wake up and find them all painted pale beige and owned by the Dutch. But I think there is now an agreement in place between the Royal Mail and English Heritage that conserves them. In the end, though, it is down to us to care about them as much as we utilize them for their vital purpose.

FROM LITTLE ACORNS

Clive Aslet
on ancient trees

ENGLAND WOULD BE NOTHING without its ancient trees. We have far more of these arboreal veterans than anywhere else in Northern Europe. Just as Trinity College, Cambridge is supposed – by Fellows of Trinity College – to contain more Nobel Prize winners than the whole of France, so Richmond Park supports more 500-year-old trees than France and Germany combined.

With our national affection for the Major Oak in Sherwood Forest, ancient cedars of Lebanon, not to mention Newton's apple tree in Lincolnshire (the tree sprouted anew after being cut down in the eighteenth century), we have been better than the Mediterranean countries at recording them. It is thought there are some ancient olive trees in Greece, but they have not achieved the degree of celebrity of, say, Sherwood's oak. We name our ancient trees. They are the subject of awe and fascination. They almost seem to speak to us, revealing something about our values and the vast span of history they have witnessed.

In Scotland, the Fortingall Yew must be one of Europe's oldest living organisms – its age calculated in millennia. Dating ancient trees is not easy: they cannot be carbon-dated because they are still growing, and the tree rings cannot be counted because they are hollow. The Fortingall Yew parted company with the original shape of its trunk long ago and now survives as a one-dimensional ligneous wall. The late Duke of Buccleuch, who had a passion for trees, made a pilgrimage to see it, saying, 'I never cease to marvel at the fact there is something living today that was 3,000 or more years old at the time of the first Christmas.'

Visiting a tree such as the Bowthorpe Oak in Lincolnshire, so hospitably big the hollow trunk was used as a dining room in the eighteenth century, makes me reach for the dictionary. Numinous is the best word I can come up with. Trees have always seemed sacred (think of the tree of Calvary, as the cross of the Crucifixion is sometimes called); their redemptive quality appears all the greater in the age of climate change, symbolizing the power of trees to redress the atmosphere's imbalance of CO_2.

Our blessing in this matter of ancient trees has little to do with our forestry. Woods do not necessarily allow trees to survive to a great age. Competition with other trees causes them to grow tall but thin, so eventually they fall. Britain's ancient trees are a legacy of the top people's passion for hunting. From the days of William the Conqueror, kings and aristocrats needed open country to ride over. This parkland included free-standing trees. Gouty and misshapen – with limbs lopped off – but with deep roots, these 'King Lears of the natural world', as Thomas Pakenham puts it, have stoically endured all that has been flung at them.

The fact they have survived into the twenty-first century has something to do with national sentiment, but more with a fact of history. Marauding armies saw them as convenient fuel, but because Britain was at peace throughout most of the eighteenth century and thereafter, its trees were spared.

Once, these trees would have enjoyed a sappy youth. They have now shrunk, as we all must, into senescence. As they collapse back into the earth, they become host to all sorts of biologically interesting intruders – the decaying timber of a dead tree is home to bats and alive with unseen invertebrates. But the most biodiverse are those still clinging tenaciously to life. Ancient trees have been called Britain's equivalent of the rainforests. And many of the most spectacular are oaks, our national tree.

RURAL RIDES

Paul Atterbury
on rural branch lines

THE VICTORIANS DID MANY good things for us – not least the building of a nationwide and fully integrated railway network. Of course, we have already undone their great work by removing much of the rural branch line experience – there is nothing better than getting off a modern mainline train at a busy station and crossing to a distant platform to board a small, usually one-car, train. I still thank our ancestors every time I find, in a quiet corner of England, that there remains a way to journey into the past, and do just that.

By 1900, about 20,000 miles of railway linked practically every town and many villages all over Britain. This meant the freedom of travel had become accessible to even people living in the most remote corners of the land. Of this dense network of lines – main lines, secondary and rural routes and branch lines – the branch lines were the most important in social terms. And there were hundreds of them all over the country, winding their way through hills and dales, mostly for a few miles but sometimes much further. They carried people to school and to work, on shopping trips, family outings and on holiday. They facilitated courting and greatly improved the national gene pool. They carried agricultural goods, materials for industry and things for the village shops. And in so doing, they – and their employees – were the heart of the communities they served.

The branch line legacy, and the society it looked after so well, lived on into the twentieth century and through two world wars. It wasn't until the 1950s that things began to change, when people and goods started to travel more by road. Left to their own devices, the railways could have responded to the challenge. But interference crept in and the old Victorian structures, which took into account social needs and benefits, and allowed the profitable main lines to subsidize the branch lines, were casually abandoned. Cost-cutting and modern efficiencies meant the rural routes and branch lines had to go. So throughout the 1960s, the axes swung and thousands of miles of railway disappeared.

For those prepared to use a map, a timetable and throw caution to the wind, the rural branch line experience is still there for the asking. By this I do not mean the preserved tourist railways. These offer a vision of railway life, but it is far better to make use of and enjoy the scattering of branch lines that somehow escaped the ravages of the 1960s and linger on in parts of Britain – still doing what they were built for in the first place.

The survivors include real branch lines, and others created by the truncation of former through routes. Cornwall has classic examples of the former, from Liskeard to Looe and from St Erth to St Ives, while East Anglia boasts an excellent couple of the latter variety, Marks Tey to Sudbury and Norwich to Sheringham. Oxfordshire has two good ones to Henley and Marlow, while elsewhere in the Midlands, the North and Wales there are exciting long branches to Matlock, Whitby and through Snowdonia to Blaenau Ffestiniog. Sadly, classic branch lines do not survive in Scotland. There is no better way to travel and see the spectacular British landscape pass by the window.

WHERE THE RIVER
MEETS THE SEA

Joan Bakewell

on estuaries

AN ESTUARY IS AN awesome thing, its great bulk of fresh water pressing forward remorselessly into the measureless ocean. It is a striking sight in all weathers – the Severn Estuary below Bristol with its rippling bore; the Mersey's quiet emergence into Liverpool Bay. But the one I really love is the gentle winding of the river Alde towards the North Sea at Aldeburgh.

Suffolk is a place admired for its vast skyscapes rather than its landscapes. The clouds scud and gather over reedy marshes and heathland – you can see the weather coming from far away and there's always time to run for cover. And a scattering of ancient spires indicates this was once a thriving centre of the wool trade. For me, however, a Suffolk scene wouldn't be as compelling without the meandering river, and the wild, unrelenting coastline with its fishermen's huts and encroaching tides.

Following the river Alde's twists and turns is like watching a drama unfold. Much of the Aldeburgh Music Festival takes place along its banks in a converted maltings – a complex of red-brick buildings sitting low in the landscape, whose steeped roofs are scarcely visible above the lie of the land. Below it, the river winds its way towards the desolate North Sea, always battling against its swaying reedbeds. On a summer evening, as the birds swoop and call above the water, it is easy to sit back, look out at the ancient Iken church alone on the horizon, and feel part of the action.

As the Alde widens its banks, the drama continues. A scattering of pine trees shed their cones on its sandy shores. At Aldeburgh itself – a one-street town whose coloured houses line the coast – the estuary turns south past a modest yacht club and finds its way to Orford, with its pretty harbour where Britten's Peter Grimes set his boats out to sea. It is hard for me to stroll along its pebble beach without hearing the opera's interludes playing in my head.

Beyond the harbour lies a sea quite unlike the Alde's meandering waterway. There is nothing gentle about this coast. The winds and tides can lash hard and the encroaching seas threaten nearby settlements. Some have already surrendered to its waves – they say further north at Dunwich you can hear the drowned church bells tolling beneath the sea. It is a place to watch distant container ships ply the world's trade and to hear the startled sounds of a beach-goer, who has ventured bravely beyond the family windbreak to test the cold water.

Of course, the Alde's days have not always been innocent. In the last wars, for example, they chose the desolate Shingle Street for military experiments. Today, oystercatchers haunt the place and visitors with binoculars come in small boats to take a look – though there isn't much to see. Change happens, history is washed away, but the Alde – with a life of its own – continues its journey to the open sea. And it is this timelessness that I believe gives the estuary its charm.

TIME TO STAND AND STARE

Muhammad Abdul Bari
on Land's End

WHEN I READ CHAPTER 31, verse 10 of the Qur'an: 'He created the heavens without any pillars . . . He placed mountains in the earth as pegs lest it should shake with you . . . He dispersed all kinds of animals . . . and sent down water from the sky causing beautiful plants to grow on it,' I think of the world's most breathtaking beauty. I think of the rural Bangladeshi village fifty miles north of the capital, where I grew up. I remain fascinated by the pristine paddy fields in the summer and the golden glow of mustard flowers in the winter. I think of the endless blue sky and the thundering clatter of monsoon rain that captivated my childhood. And I think of the year I first came to Britain and fell in love with rural England.

My career in the Bangladesh Air Force brought me to Britain for about a year in the late 1970s to train with the RAF College Cranwell, in Lincolnshire. And when I later came back to Britain to study for a PhD in physics, I always enjoyed taking my family out of London to explore the country's rural areas. My love of beautiful mountains and open seas took us to many coastal locations. But nothing fascinated me more than Land's End – the tip of England in the mighty Atlantic Ocean.

Situated about ten miles from Penzance in Cornwall, Land's End is magnificent. Even with the vast ocean on three sides, it still manages to make its mark – rather than engulfing it, the giant Atlantic has taken it in its lap. Its granite cliffs are fascinating, but dangerous. And although you cannot see what lies beyond the horizon, on a clear day you can just about make out the Isles of Scilly – a cluster of small, lovely islands – and Longships Lighthouse. When the summer sunshine beams down on the water and the mild wind blows inland from the ocean, there's nowhere I'd rather be.

The first time I stood up on the tip of the hill in front of this endless expanse of water, it rendered me speechless. I was struck by how the power of the ocean and the strength of the cliffs can reduce you to a mere spectator of nature – a tiny observer of the cosmos. It is a place that takes you momentarily away from the constraints of life and makes you question the futility of your existence. Even the seabirds seem more worthy in this magical environment. Visitors come here to get away from it all, but it's a place where I feel you can learn more about yourself as you stare out across the ocean. You may be small in comparison, but it is here – where daily life is surrendered to the elements – that you can really find yourself.

For many intrepid walkers keen to explore the Cornish coastal path, this end of our land marks the beginning of a journey – the gateway to other places of outstanding beauty. Those who take to the neighbouring cliffs will join the longest continuous footpath in Britain, covering the coast from Poole Harbour through Dorset to Somerset and the Bristol Channel – and passing wonderful locations such as Sennen Cove to the north. It is a romantic and truly delightful path of discovery.

I wish everyone – especially young Muslim people from inner cities – could experience such unrivalled beauty. It is a beauty that would, no doubt, enable them to strike their roots more firmly in this soil.

SIGHTING THE STUBBLE-STAG

Simon Barnes
on hares

I WAS ON A horse, the best kind of hide; make use of one and at a stroke, you are an honorary quadruped. As a result, the rabbit didn't break cover till I was right on top of him. And then it changed. Transfigured. Metamorphosed before my eyes.

It is one of the countryside's loveliest conjuring tricks. The rabbit rose on four hydraulic rams and became an antelope. Instead of going hoppity-hop, he shifted into an unsparing Serengeti gallop, back level, head still, mighty levers pounding the ground at bewildering speed, in sight for long seconds across the just-harvested field.

The stubble-stag, the stook-deer, the stag sprouting a suede horse, the creature living in the corn . . . this from *The Names of the Hare*, as translated from the Middle English by Seamus Heaney, for a hare it was, all right. It is hard to vanish in Suffolk; the place has too much sky, so the hare has speed instead. He was in sight, but out of reach, and getting more out of reach at a steady forty-five mph. About twice the speed of Usain Bolt. A hare was once seen jumping a Grand National fence.

The Easter bunny is a hare, for it was believed that hares laid eggs in open fields. Well, when the stook-deer takes off at the speed of light and you find a lapwing's nest in the place he has vanished from, what's a chap to think? Bugs Bunny is a hare too. American jackrabbits are a species of hare: they produce good-to-go babies above the ground, instead of blind, naked mewlings in a hole.

There were once four million hares in this country, there are now about 80,000. About half of them live in Suffolk, Norfolk and Cambridgeshire, they prefer the dry side of the country. Under the government-sponsored Biodiversity Action Plan, the population of hares was supposed to double by 2010. It hasn't.

Hares are too scarce, but they still fire the English imagination. People sculpt them and paint them obsessively. Many people – often those who have never seen a real one – claim hares as their favourite animals. Hares are seldom seen, but a single sighting goes very deep. And in part, at least, that comes from this ability to metamorphose. That transition from being an overlooked rabbit to a hare you can't take your eyes from, is one of the wild world's routine pieces of magic.

Other transmutations, other metamorphoses: the swift that is suddenly uncommonly large, becoming a hobby, the most elegant falcon in creation . . . the group of cliff-edge tumbling jackdaws that, in an instant, acquire fire-red beaks and become choughs . . . the white butterfly that acquires a miraculous glow and becomes the year's first male orange-tip.

And then there is the thicket that suddenly explodes with the song of nightingale, the bracken frond that shifts uncannily and becomes an adder, or the patch of sea that turns into a Brobdingnagian hat and produces not a rabbit, or even a hare, but a school of dolphins. At a stroke your perception of the world changes, the world itself changes.

The world makes a transition from ordinary to special; from mundane to marvellous; from commonplace to miraculous. We are often told that there are marvels all around us: how very nice it is when a hare takes the trouble to show us.

'SUMMER IS ICUMEN IN'

Laura Barton

on a traditional English round

THE THING I HAVE always loved about England is its wildness, its unbridled vigour and fire and ruggedness, it is there in our language and our landscape, our manner and our music. And if there's a song that embodies this national spirit I have always believed it to be 'Summer Is Icumen In'. A traditional English round, thought to date from around 1260, its thirteen lines are written in Middle English, more particularly the Wessex dialect. It begins with a resounding shout: 'Summer has come in,/Loudly sing, cuckoo!' it declares. 'The seed grows and the meadow blooms/And the wood springs anew,/Sing, cuckoo!'

Sometimes known as the Reading Rota, it hails from the Reading Abbey manuscript, though its author is unknown. Speculation, nonetheless, has placed it at the feet of W. de Wycombe, an English composer of the period, best known for his polyphonic alleluias. 'Summer Is Icumen In' is one of the earliest instances of counterpoint and also one of the first examples of a piece of music with both religious and secular lyrics — though the sacred version, in Latin, concerns the Crucifixion rather than the arrival of the summer and the song of the cuckoo. The piece is written for four voices, joined at the interchanges by two deeper voices, and its melody is both one of the oldest-known illustrations of the major mode and the oldest example of ground-bass — though such terminology communicates very little of the song's vibrancy, its light-footed joy.

Its subject is springtime and the great unfurling ecstasy of the English countryside in that season, a time when, as the song puts it, 'The ewe bleats after the lamb/The cow lows after the calf./The bullock stirs, the stag farts.' There is a real lusty fervour to 'Summer Is Icumen In', and it is this quality that has always made me think that this song seems a glorious precursor to rock 'n' roll — they are both, after all, concerned with sex and noise and the sheer joy of being alive.

That it is sung in the round brings a glorious tumbling quality to these lyrics, a sound that mimics the delights of the season here in England, when the fierce green buds unwind and spread, the hedgerows spill over, and the frozen stream thaws and begins its chuckling run. When all is noise and bluster and fluttering, and the birds swoop low and call out their own tunes over and over – 'Merrily sing, cuckoo!' as the song holds it, 'Cuckoo, cuckoo, well you sing, cuckoo.' It is in this celebration of new life returning, and the infinite structure of the round, that 'Summer Is Icumen In' instills its message. Life will always begin once more, it seems to say. It is an endless round, and the song will always play on: 'Don't you ever stop now,' it runs. 'Sing, cuckoo, now. Sing, cuckoo./Sing, cuckoo. Sing, cuckoo, now!'

THROUGH THE LYCHGATE

Sister Wendy Beckett
on country churchyards

OPEN THE LYCHGATE AND walk up the path to the church door. Almost certainly, you will find it locked. But all around the church is another sacred space, the churchyard where all who have prayed within the walls of this church, over the centuries, have been laid to rest.

This is consecrated ground, as holy in its own way as the church itself. Listen to its peace. The dark bulk of yew trees protects it, and a churchyard seems to have a silence uniquely its own. It is not a garden, with flower beds, but a yard, and the only flowers are wild flowers in the corners, and a few that are heaped on recent graves. There will be a mowing rota for the parish, and the grass rolls smoothly over the unevenness that covers the unmarked graves.

Tombstones stand in lines, or are dotted haphazardly, some erect, some leaning, but most of the villagers would not have been able to afford such a thing. When they were first laid in this blessed soil, back in the fourteenth, fifteenth, sixteenth centuries, they would have been marked by a small wooden cross which has long ago crumbled to dust. Even those who were marked by a gravestone are mostly no longer identifiable. The words so lovingly chiselled can no longer be read. Water and wind have eroded them, and there is a marvellous array of lichens decorating the stone. This is an unpolluted place, and so there are more rare mosses and lichens in churchyards such as this than anywhere else in the country. It is unpolluted in every sense, a silent, gentle place where all those who have prayed in the church, longed and doubted, rejoiced and feared, now rest bodily 'in sure and certain hope of the Resurrection'.

The lychgate through which we entered has a small roof to it. 'Lych' is the Anglo-Saxon word for corpse, and here the villagers would bring the body, resting it at the gate while the priest came from the church to accompany it to the grave. Medieval dead had no coffins, merely winding sheets, and there was a much greater physical intimacy with the dead than we know in our more sanitized and impersonal day.

There was also a much greater certainty that the corpse was merely the less important bodily aspect of the beloved relative or friend who was being buried. Something of this long-sustained faith seems to have imbued the churchyard. When Thomas Gray wrote his famous poem, 'Elegy Written in a Country Churchyard' his interest was almost wholly in the men (he mentions no women) whom he describes as 'the rude forefathers of the hamlet'. He makes no mention of faith. It is their lives of what he describes as 'useful toil' and 'homely joys' that interest him: 'the short and simple annals of the poor'.

From meditating on the necessary end of all lives, whether simple or splendid, Gray moves, in typical eighteenth-century fashion, to meditating upon himself. He imagines that he will die young and obscure (both suppositions happily mistaken), and produces his own epitaph. There are, it is true, countless unknown stories of the people who lie buried here, but imagining their lives or brooding on their deaths seems a rather overactive preoccupation for a quiet time standing beneath the 'yew tree's shade'. There is a benison in the very stillness of the churchyard, but we must be still ourselves, with quiet minds, to receive it.

GHOST ORCHIDS

Antony Beevor
on the world of Jocelyn Brooke

WE LIVE RIGHT IN the heart of Jocelyn Brooke's country, south-east of Canterbury, a comparatively small area of chalk downland between the Elham and Pett valleys. Brooke, a botanist specializing in orchids who became an acclaimed novelist, lived at Bishopsbourne, less than three miles away.

Brooke worked for years on *The Wild Orchids of Britain* (finally published in 1952), but he only began to achieve recognition after the war, when he merged his botanical interests with lyrical, semi-fictional memories of childhood. Anthony Powell, one of his greatest admirers, was taken by his Proustian approach to nostalgia. Brooke's novels also contained a strong homoerotic subtext, which terrified his publishers in that repressive age. This was frequently expressed in his loving descriptions of the rare orchids, such as the lizard, monkey and bee orchids, which he sought on his long rambles. He was fascinated by the phallic military orchid, which became the title of his first published novel. Brooke's love affair with a soldier from the Seaforth Highlanders, based near Dover, is conveyed in this book in a vivid but veiled prose.

Other orchids, like the large white lady orchid, appear from time to time in our wood and fields. One year, we even had ten at once. But apart from common spotted and pyramidal orchids, many varieties have decreased. This is largely due to the gradual change from traditional sheep-grazing to horse paddocks, as the countryside switches from agriculture to 'leisure activities', or what the Italians call *agri-turismo*. Sadly, the marked increase in the number of horses on bridleways and in fields has led to a noticeable reduction of the orchid population.

Brooke would certainly regret that decline, yet these downlands and valleys have changed astonishingly little, mainly because the roads are so narrow and villages of any size so far apart. This has prevented the area from becoming commuter land, even with the great increase in the size of our two nearest towns, Ashford and Canterbury. Those high-banked, close-hedged little roads, often with grass growing down the middle, and a lack of signposts reminiscent of the summer of 1940 when they were taken down to confuse possible German paratroops, seem to deter many urban-minded folk. But also, for reasons I have never understood, but still bless, the strip of Kent between the M2 and M20 motorways has avoided the suburban spread of many other parts of the county. Maidstone and Ashford have increased to the south of the M20, while Canterbury and Faversham have widened to the north of the M2. Each spring, the bluebell woods of beech, sweet chestnut and hazel, and the primrose-banked hedgerows of hawthorn, field maple and hornbeam bring back Brooke's 'private kingdom'.

Less than half a mile from our gate, a favourite walk takes us past an isolated half-timbered house at Clambercrown, which used to be a pub called the Dog. It will long be remembered, I hope, as the title of Brooke's most admired novel, *The Dog at Clambercrown*. Brooke, a melancholic and acutely self-conscious individual, found his escape in writing and his love of wild flowers. Nobody has evoked the scenery and atmosphere of that corner of the North Downs better. The miracle is that it has survived largely unscathed.

THE CALL OF THE GROUSE

David Bellamy

on grouse moors

'GO BACK! GO BACK!' is the call of Britain's only endemic bird that thrives along with over sixty million people in the mix of landscapes that Winston Churchill said 'was worth dying for'. These landscapes were people-made and people-managed long before the internal combustion engine made it easier to plough, sow, reap, mow and fell trees to make room for grazing animals and growing crops to feed people.

The rot set in when Stone Age immigrants discovered what we now call the Lake District and a very useful greenstone. This they quarried, worked and polished to produce axe heads strong and keen enough to fell the ancient forests that then covered most of these isles.

Long before this the post-glacial hunter-gatherers had found hunting no easy matter for the trees got in the way of giving chase. So it was that a mere 5,000 years after the end of the last Ice Age, slash and burn became the principal behind the foundation of our most cherished natural landscapes.

With the development of bronze and iron tools the removal of trees and scrub was easier, and with warmer and wetter weather massive leaching and erosion of soil took their toll. Our uplands suffered worst and soon became covered with acidic moorland and blanketed with peat, devoid of trees and bushes. This created my chosen icon, the ideal habitat for the grouse.

As the little Ice Age began to come to an end in the Nineteenth Century, the rising temperature and the increase in the amount of carbon dioxide and oxides of nitrogen in cycle (both of which are plant fertilisers) boosted the growth of trees, once again threatening the very existence of the open vistas that are the multicoloured backbone of Britain.

Fortunately the grouse moors were already being managed by regular burning to provide a patchwork of different-aged heather stands, food, cover and shelter for the grouse and many other special creatures great and small. I salute the gamekeepers who work their magic come rain or shine to this day, they are practical conservationists without equal.

Red grouse, found naturally only in Britain, are ground dwellers and so are at the mercy of all types of predators from golden eagles to foxes. Thanks to good parenthood, camouflage and take-off prowess they exploited the habitat well until sporting shotguns evolved from the fowling piece, and the sporting gentleman became another predator that joined the pack: complete with a well-trained dog and a loader, he would walk the moor in what was reckoned to be the quintessential art of the hunt.

The main food of this wonderful bird is heather, the young regrowth shoots of which are densely packed and rich in nutrients. The only other input required is a soupçon of daddy-long-legs and there are plenty of them about, along with other creepy crawlies, proving that if the management is good the natural history of one of the world's rarest ecosystems is not imperilled.

Another moorland crop that creates jobs and cash flow is the product of the heather honey bee, all in tune with the sweetest buzz of biodiversity.

In the blooming pink of high summer there is little to beat the spectacle of a grouse moor. A worthy icon, providing the best of free range cordon pink game while ensuring that there will, still, be the best heather honey for tea.

LET'S TALK ABOUT THE WEATHER

Floella Benjamin
on the English climate

THE FIRST THING I noticed, as the ship neared the end of its four-thousand-mile journey from my homeland of Trinidad, was the insidious chill which penetrated the flimsy party dress I wore for my arrival in the Land of Hope and Glory, England; the land I had been taught in school to love from afar. I stood shivering on the deck of the steamer as it nosed its way into the docks at Southampton on 1 September, 1960. This was my first impression of England, the coldness. My mother, who had travelled ahead to England fifteen months earlier, waited on the dockside with woolly jumpers to cosset her precious children. She had come prepared, for she had learnt the vagaries of the English weather. 'All the English people seem to talk about is the weather,' she used to say. Even after fifty years living here, she would still say it and she was right, there was plenty of it to talk about.

As our train sped out of Southampton towards the gaunt, grey buildings of London, I was intoxicated by the greenness of the countryside. Nothing had prepared me for the variety of the constantly changing landscapes which rushed by, and the vision is still etched on my mind. The lush fields flaunting different shades of green, bounded by towering woodland, each tree with its own shade of emerald, already tinged with the early gold of autumn. The rolling hills that bore them reminded me of a green patchwork quilt.

Although Trinidad is covered in evergreen rainforest, laced with colourful tropical flowers, the grassland is mostly singed fawn by the relentless blaze of the sun, only turning pale green during the rainy season when a warm, sensual, rain you can dance in buckets briefly down. This is quite unlike the thin, incessant, icy rain I discovered falling from the dark, brooding English clouds.

As the weeks passed, my siblings and I got used to the cold, which increased as autumn fully claimed the landscape, covering the streets with a dense carpet of golden leaves. Yes, the streets were paved with gold as we had been told, but not the kind of precious gold we had all expected. Winter drew rapidly in and the trees curiously lost their leaves, exposing the branches like skeletons reaching for the sky.

As the frosty air gripped harder, I was fascinated by the smoke that billowed out of my mouth as I exhaled. I thought there was a fire within my chest as I blew the smoke out like a dragon.

Smog, caused by the dense coal smoke that spewed out of the chimneys which looked like soldiers guarding the slated rooftops, crept through the streets, cutting visibility down dramatically. It created a ghostly atmosphere with people moving mysteriously through the sullen grey mist like wraiths in a horror film.

Yes, in my short time in England, I certainly experienced many different types of weather. But the morning I awoke to find my room filled with an eerie clear light and muffled silence is something I will never forget. I rushed to the window and wiped the condensation caused by our paraffin heater from the pane. What I saw thrilled me and took my breath away. A pure whiteness dazzled me and gave me the sensation of being in another world. Everything was covered in a thick fluffy blanket of fresh snow!

I had seen snow on Christmas cards back in Trinidad, but standing there, looking at its clean, white, magical beauty in amazement, my heart soared and, at that moment, I fell in love with snow.

I have lived in Britain now for fifty years and I still find myself sighing with joy as the landscape changes and seasons unfold, each one with its own special character. Spring, its cherry blossom dancing in the breeze with a promise of lazy afternoons of English tea on the lawn. Showery summers mingled with scarce hot, sunny cricket days. Autumn with its blaze of glorious colour slowly unfolding before, once again, winter inexorably clenches its icy fist, and the cycle renews.

Devouring the relentless miles whilst training for my marathons, I am inspired as I absorb the essences of each new season. And in my role as President of the Ramblers' Association I find inner peace as I walk through England's mountains green, as goes that great hymn I learnt as a child back in Trinidad.

Yes, to my surprise, I have grown to love the English weather in all its forms, and miss it when I'm away . . . even the coldness!

SENSES AND SENSIBILITY

Richard Benson
on rural sensuality

ONE BRIGHT BLUE, OVEN-HOT afternoon in the summer of 1984, my friend Johnny and I were constructing the top layers of a vast straw stack in a field on the East Yorkshire Wolds. We were eighteen, and working for a local farmer in our last school summer holiday. All our summers were spent in this way, but for some reason I have a clear memory of this particular day, or rather of a particular moment in it.

It came as we finished unloading a trailerful of bales. As the straw stack was close to a windbreak of larch, damson and apple trees, we pulled some apples from the branches and sat on the straw to eat them. They were unripe, bitter-tasting Bramleys, but eating them up there in the sunshine felt good. We experienced one of those small stretches of serenity that always seem to come over you in the countryside when you are least expecting them. I remember that, instead of insulting each other, or arguing, or talking about pop music, we just sat in happy silence for about a quarter of an hour. It's hard to explain more than that, except perhaps to say that it was as if in eating the apples we had swallowed part of the glorious afternoon.

When I think now of the fifteen or so minutes we lay on top of the stack, I have a recollection of our surroundings that is disarmingly vivid. The faint wind – warm from the baking Wolds – on my face; the leafy stir of trees around the stack; the slightly sour, earthy odour of barley straw and the virile green scent of summer verges that one almost tastes. Apart from the nursery-blue sky with its infant thunderclouds, though, there is no meaningful visual element to this memory. I think this is telling, and I mention it here because I think it is easy to forget the powerful sensuality of the English countryside and the impression it can make on us.

Fortunately, you do not have to lie on top of a straw stack to experience this. It suffices to simply walk down a green lane, stop and close your eyes for a full minute. Listen, smell, feel, suck the air in, and the place enters into you in a way that it cannot when you merely stand admiring a view. Marvellous vistas are all very well, but looking at them can make you feel separate from the landscape; how often do you hear someone say that a view looks 'unreal', or that they 'cannot take it in'? In contrast, although we may be barely conscious of what our other four senses are registering, it is often via these sensations that we viscerally cognize the countryside when we are in it.

The English landscape has a distinctive ease and quiet luxuriance. It is generally moist, lush and soft, with ample curves and sibilance; its weather does not punish with extremes; our wildlife is pretty, timid and unthreatening. It has its celebrated all-time-classic sensations, such as the smell of fresh hay, the cawing of rooks and the feel of sea spray, but the dearest are likely to be personal.

Those I would take to my boring, dry desert island include the fragrance of peas harvested on a summer evening; the foot-feel of frozen mud ruts under your boots on an early January morning and the keening of an invisible light aircraft, pleasant because it highlights the silence. I might also add the taste of wild fruit – chiefly in memory of that perfect moment from my childhood.

Talking about it years later, Johnny and I agreed that it was probably the first time we became fully aware of the infinite, indifferent splendour of the countryside. This might seem strange, given that we had grown up there, but it isn't really. Those most familiar with a place can be the slowest to understand it – particularly if they think too much about what it looks like.

STICKING THE WICKET

Scyld Berry

on village cricket

CRICKET FIGURES LARGELY IN the English rural idyll. Not so celebrated is the sport's role in achieving social cohesion, in preventing the warp and weft of English – and British – life from becoming unravelled.

Let me introduce you to T—. It is a large village in the old North Somerset coalfield. The quality of housing stock is pretty ordinary, as you would expect it to be, given its historical background and the inequality of English society through the ages. Romantic-sounding though some names in this part of Somerset can be, there is plenty of roughness and violence.

I was going to continue referring to this place as T—, I still play cricket against them, and I am too far past the age for batting to cope with a bouncer or beamer if one of their fast bowlers wants to take it out on me next season.

But there is nothing here for anyone to be ashamed of or embarrassed about. This village is called Timsbury, and their cricket team has reached a Cup Final at Lord's, which is more than mine has done.

The playing fields are at the heart of Timsbury, which is where they should be. They are big enough to have two football pitches; in summer, one cricket pitch with generous boundaries. A clubhouse with dressing rooms on the ground floor accommodates the players of both sports, and on the upper level is a bar and space for teas.

After playing against Timsbury a few times over the years, my guess – and not even a fully qualified sociologist could prove anything either way – is that the cricket and football clubs have done a lot for the social cohesion there.

Their cricket team is always full of young lads – lads who would have to spend their weekends in other ways if they did not have access to this green open space and, of course, to the adult volunteers who provide them with an infrastructure.

The highest annual homicide rate in England has been achieved – if that is the word – by more than one community in the West Country. Timsbury, I bet, will never be a candidate for this distinction so long as cricket and football are played there. More likely, they will produce a bowler who is too quick for me . . .

And the latest good news is that Timsbury has been given a grant by the England and Wales Cricket Board for a second cricket ground.

A PERSONAL VIEW

Harold 'Dickie' Bird
on Scarborough

SCARBOROUGH IS A VERY special place to me. I have been fortunate enough to visit many parts of the world and nowhere matches this favourite Yorkshire resort and its immediate surrounding coastline. Only on the east coast of New Zealand have I found comparable charm, but, in the end, Scarborough is still tops.

My love affair with the town started in my childhood, when, as was common everywhere in the industrial north, families went to the seaside for an annual holiday – just a week in those days. My parents, sister and I went to Scarborough for our break. The annual exodus from Barnsley was a great British tradition.

So, what makes Scarborough so special? For me, and not unsurprisingly for someone with my background, it's the Cricket Festival. This, until very recently, has always been played at the end of the season, and it was in 2001 that I was present when Yorkshire clinched the County Championship here. It was the county's first title in thirty-three years, and 14,000 people had packed into North Marine Road to see the victory against Glamorgan. It was forty-two years since I had been a member of a Yorkshire Championship side, and I had yet to take up my umpiring career when the last victory in 1968 had been achieved.

Also, it was announced that I was to be President of the Festival the following season. It was indeed an honour to follow such great names as Sir Leonard Hutton, Sir Donald Bradman, Sir Paul Getty and, most recently, my old pal Sir Michael Parkinson. And it was all the better for starting my term of office with Yorkshire as County Champions!

But Scarborough has so much more. It is home to my favourite fish and chip shop, the Small Fry in North Street. It is only a small place, as the name suggests, but it has a big reputation. I used to eat my fish and chips out of the paper, but now, in my retirement, I sit in the café and dine in comfort.

Scarborough has wonderful views from both its bays, with the remains of the historic castle dominating the headland between the two. The castle was an important part of east coast defences in times gone by, and is now frequented by visitors interested in its history. Given glorious weather, there is nowhere to touch the British Isles, and when you gaze over a panorama like the one at Scarborough from its famous castle, it's simply breathtaking.

In addition to its history and great beauty, Scarborough also has everything associated with the traditional British seaside holiday. Cockles and mussels on the promenade; ice creams; amusement arcades and bingo halls when the weather is less kind; donkey rides on the sands; and deckchairs for relaxation. It has one of the best beaches in the country and I look on enviously now that I can no longer join in the many games of beach cricket which are played, together with other traditional sports. It's good to see youngsters playing sport, rather than being glued to technology or standing on street corners. This is something I have tried to encourage through my foundation, the purpose of which is to help and encourage young people to play sport and hopefully enjoy it as much as I did. And finally, if you just want to take life easy, as I often do these days, the town has its long-standing establishments such as the Spa Pavilion, where you can sit and listen to the resident music trio or some other band.

So there it is. Scarborough, the complete seaside town – history, charm and beauty mixed with holiday favourites. Something for everyone and all done in style. No wonder that I have been there every year since my retirement and intend to continue to do so for many more years!

AN ORDINARY BEAUTY

Terence Blacker
on Lonely Road

OUTSIDE THE VILLAGE OF Dickleburgh in the Waveney Valley of south Norfolk, there is a narrow lane called Lonely Road. After a few hundred yards, it becomes a footpath which leads past a farmhouse and a row of allotments. There, at the end of the track, the path grows narrower and enters a stretch of woodland which forms a sort of passageway into the landscape. When you emerge, you find yourself in the kind of landscape for which this part of England is so well loved – open, undulating farmland, with small woods dividing the fields under a big Norfolk sky. In winter, you are likely to see flocks of golden plovers and lapwings which regularly visit these fields; in summer, the sound of skylark song will be in the air.

This place has a history – it was once the site of Pulham Air Station, from where the first transatlantic crossing by air balloon took place – but its present is more important. Today Lonely Road offers the residents of the four villages nearby, of which I am one, the chance to enjoy a landscape uncluttered by pylons, masts, roads or railways. Its ordinary beauty is something we have taken for granted down the years.

Only when a local planning officer recently referred to the 'unexceptional quality of the landscape' did ordinariness become a problem. The planner was supporting an application for a wind-measuring mast. By the time this book is published, the fields surrounding Lonely Road may well be on the way to becoming definitively cluttered. Thanks to the determined efforts of a landowner and the opportunism of a developer, there is a plan to place three 130-metre wind turbines on the fields.

So our little community, like many others across Britain, finds itself caught up in the great national debate about the future of the planet. It is difficult to convey how unpleasant and, above all, how strange the experience has been. Those of us who agree that a shift to renewable energy is essential, but that global need does not justify the sacrifice of much-loved countryside, are regularly portrayed as villainous and selfish – we are the equivalent of drink-drivers, one government minister has said. Landowners and developers whose only motive is financial are suddenly heroes of the environment. Politicians, speaking to a largely urban electorate, have discovered that wind turbines are an easy vote-winner, symbols of green concern which will be viewed by the vast majority only on TV screens or on holiday.

What chance has our little patch of 'unexceptional' landscape against the might of environmental correctness? To those who do not enjoy or understand the countryside – like most politicians, one suspects – the idea that a few fields and birds, a bit of woodland, can be set against a great global concern will seem bizarre. Yet, as they become increasingly rare, these unspoilt, ordinary places matter, each in its own particular way. The fields outside Dickleburgh, for example, offer an unusual variety of birdlife, access to nature and rural peace for hundreds of villagers. The great abstract ideals of environmentalism mean nothing when they are achieved against the grain of local environments.

It is difficult, walking down Lonely Road, not to be saddened by the concrete and steel nightmare which may well lie ahead. In years to come, when the ugly remains of greed and political panic litter the landscape – the true icons of early twenty-first-century Britain – future generations may wonder what on earth possessed their parents and grandparents to give up so easily what is so precious.

LOVE'S LABOURS WON

Raymond Blanc

on orchards

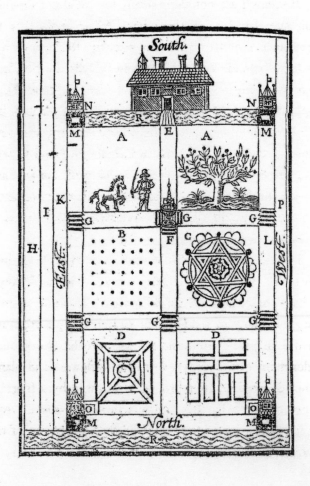

BEING A CHEF, IT'S easy for me to think of food when I consider the landscape of this, my adopted country. But I also think of something that flourishes in the gentle, moderate climate; something that leaves its mark for generations, but is also up to date and always in need of renewal; something we have to tend for future generations. I think of apples and orchards.

It seems I am not alone in my love of this fruit-filled landscape. In *Julius Caesar*, Shakespeare highlights the importance of orchards when he discusses the legacy a man can leave behind. When Mark Antony tells the people of Rome the contents of Caesar's will (act III, scene II), he emphasizes the orchards Caesar ordered to be planted: 'He hath left you all his walks/His private arbours, and new-planted orchards . . . he hath left them you/And to your heirs for ever; common pleasures/To walk abroad, and recreate yourselves.' For Shakespeare, orchards were places to be admired and enjoyed – something I have tried to recreate in Great Milton.

In the grounds of Le Manoir – in the fold of hills that overlook the water meadows of the Thames Valley – we have the remains of an old orchard. It is only a small plot, and many of its wizened Bramley apple trees are too old to give their best. So we have let the ground under many of the trees revert to wild flowers and plants – snowdrops first, then crocuses, followed by a fragrant carpet of bluebells. It's glorious in every season, from the first greening of the buds and the appearance of the lemony primroses, to the blossom and the humming of the thriving insect population in the dried grasses of late autumn.

This wonderful scene affords us our 'common pleasures'. But we know that, to provide something practical for future generations to enjoy, we can't just create a beautiful space. So as well as the tiny show orchard, we are now planting a twenty-acre apple and pear orchard. We are also adding something completely new but not out of character for the site – a lavender-bounded Provençal orchard with apricots and figs.

The fifty varieties of apple and pear we plan to use are yet to be decided. But I'm certain we'll have some of the best older local varieties, especially the greatest Oxfordshire cultivar, the Blenheim orange. This large, solid, crisp green apple – with its blush of red and haunting perfume – is stunningly good either raw or cooked, but difficult to buy, even locally. The trees are magnificent in stature, which makes them unsuitable for modern systems of training. This means a mixture of systems will be used in our new orchard. Whatever we decide, we know that we will be enhancing the landscape – not just for us, but for our heirs for ever.

Apple- (and pear-) growing is one of the things England does best. And the simple act of choosing an English apple – over, say, a Chinese one grown in almost unthinkably large quantities – is a vote for biodiversity, as well as the preservation of our own traditional landscape. Old pearmain, recorded in the thirteenth century, is probably the only one of our contemporary English apples that Shakespeare would have recognized. But he'd agree that the names of the cultivars are themselves poetic. Ashmead's kernel, Brownlees, Russet, Ellison's orange, King of the pippins, Laxton's fortune, Lord Lambourne, Pitmaston pineapple, and Ribston pippin are just some of the delectable choices on offer to help us give something back to our region and its countryside.

THOSE SPECIAL PLACES

Ronald Blythe
on privately claimed territories

WE WERE DRIVING ALONG the lane leading to the fields which we crossed to Vicarage Cottage, Grandmother's house, when I suddenly noticed it, the hitching post. And after all these years. And painted white, with the iron ring which as a boy I never passed without lifting, and then letting it fall. We stopped and I did it once more. These rituals are not uncommon. Dr Johnson, the rational giant, had his normally erratic progress further impeded by not stepping on the line between flagstones. Eventually, such compulsions create a private landscape, one of deep experiences and revelation. A holiday long ago is whittled down to a single memory, such as lying on the thrift at Land's End and being lulled into teenage fatalism by the marvellously dull regularity of the crashing waters below. Once I returned to sit again on the very spot. In Perthshire I accidentally witnessed an aged friend making her farewell to a deserted village on Rannoch Moor, going the rounds, touching the broken crofts as she had done as a schoolgirl, when the holidays were over. But now she was touching them for the last time, as she would not be able to manage the rough walk through the heather again.

I haven't dared to paddle in the shallow stream which feeds the Stour, as this would be too much for the passers-by. But it was where the tiny fish hurried between my white water-extended feet and the sand whirled between my toes. As most of us children splashed there, a good many old chaps and women may well have this summer ditch on their personal map. Not so the ancient, uncomfortable wall against which I was pressed to be kissed, and which I nod to en route to Waitrose.

Wildflower and wildfruit sites are extant here and there. Human beings are apt to have a weird kind of vanity about certain species blushing unseen by them, and I would experience guilt if I suddenly remembered the white violets, only to find them over. People would tell each other, 'The white violets are out!' and I would go at once to 'my' patch. It was near the frogspawn pond, a place I had long annexed. Not long ago, a neighbour said, 'You must come and see our pond,' and I was almost driven to state my earlier claim. The poet John Clare laid claim to everything which grew, flew or simply *was* in his native village, making bird lists and flower inventories, as well as recording all the neighbours' shouts and songs, although privatizing them at the same time, and making them sacred to him. These folk and plants, these footpaths and roads, may have been redistributed by an Enclosure Act, but history has proved that no countryside can be seen in the general sense after it has been through the private lens of a great local writer.

But the majority of us do not list our private acres, our plane tree in St James's Park, our little consoling geographies which have been brought about by love or maybe by just sheltering from the rain. Smells come into mine. The promising odour when I open the door of an old church which is the same concoction as that I knew when I was prying around Perp and Dec* in my twenties, and persists in spite of decades of the latest cleansers and flower arrangements. A whiff of something which is doctrinal as much as bats and books. I breathe it in thankfully, the

* Perpendicular and Decorated are styles of church architecture.

irremediable dust which is mine alone and part of my most intimate history, be it released in a nave in Cornwall or Powys. How did this strong scent of ages get out of my native Suffolk? But what a comfort that it did. For I can have it anywhere I go. Even in France.

I have never made a pilgrimage to any of my privately claimed territories, for this is what these cliffs, woods, churchyards, fields, occasional London streets, wildflower sites, ditches, rivers and lonely beaches are, places which hold the kind of information which is difficult enough for me to find, let alone a biographer. I have been a notorious loller in the sun, listener in the wind, watcher of small events, determined wanderer around, and adventurer in my way. Now and then I turn up where I practised, like Samuel Johnson, absurd rituals, or where sea sound overwhelmed me (Hoy), or mostly where I daydreamed. Did my parked bike leave its mark on a rock? One of the earliest things I can recall is leaving a lead soldier under a fat flint in a cobbled yard. Why? To preserve him? To lose him? 'What a strange boy,' they would have said, had I told them. But it is not until this moment that it has occurred to me, via the hitching post, that I have spread myself widely and secretly, as have most of us. Worse – or better – I have been fetishistic, curious and enquiring. And much alone in the open air.

MY LITTLE PIECE OF HISTORY

Rosie Boycott
on fossils

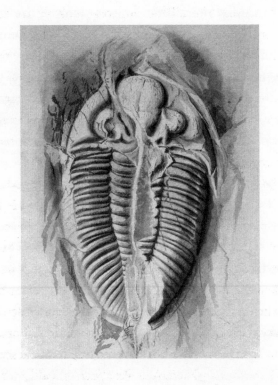

Mary Anning's fossil shop lies halfway down Broad Street in Lyme Regis. If you're looking downhill towards the sea, the shop is on the right, at a point on the street where the pavement is raised above the level of the road and a shiny black railing stops you from accidentally falling on to the cars below. For most people, Lyme's claim to fame is as the location for John Fowles' *The French Lieutenant's Woman*. Walk down to the finger-shaped pier – known locally as the Cobb – and on any day of the year there'll be someone looking out to sea, the wind blowing the hair off their face, mimicking Meryl Streep as she appeared in the closing frames of the film. But the town's most honoured individual should rightfully be Mary Anning. She didn't sign any declarations or fight any battles, but down along the cliffs which converge on Lyme Regis she made a discovery that changed her world – and ours.

Mary Anning's life would make a rather spectacular movie. When she was a fifteen-month-old baby, it is reported that a lightning bolt struck her and the three older girls taking care of her. Only Mary survived. Her father was a cabinetmaker who liked to take his young daughter on trips to look at the 'curiosities' embedded in the local cliffs. He died when Mary was eleven, leaving the family destitute. So Mary started selling the fossils to Victorian visitors, who came to Lyme to enjoy its bracing air and dramatic scenery. In 1811 she found what looked like a four-foot alligator skull in the cliffs. With her brother's help she gently removed it from its 150-million-year-old tomb. A storm did the rest, revealing the full skeleton of the first ichthyosaurus the world had ever seen.

Today Mary's shop is packed full of fossils from all over the world. Whenever I go there I buy another local, polished ammonite – a thin slice of wonder that fits neatly into the pocket of my jeans. A small gold label attached to the boxes in which the fossils sit tells me they have been found on the Jurassic Coast and are 170 million years old. They cost just £2.50. And it's this that I really can't get over. For £2.50 I can buy, say, nine cigarettes or the polished remains of a cephalopod mollusc (a relative of the squid and octopus family), which lived round Lyme Regis an unimaginably long time ago. Ammonites were free-swimming creatures that used the chambers in their shells as ballast tanks to control their buoyancy. They disappeared about sixty million years ago – around the time the dinosaurs became extinct.

I like giving ammonites away to people, and I like to keep one in my bag or in my pocket. I take it out sometimes and just stare at its lovely spiral pattern, a pattern that has never been bettered in millions of years. Like the patterns of a seashell, or the arrangement of leaves on a sunflower, my ammonites conform to the Fibonacci number system. This simple system ($1 + 1 = 2$, $2 + 1 = 3$ and so on) results in the Golden Number, or the Golden Ratio, which caused such a deep philosophical crisis among mathematicians of the fifth century BC as they first grappled with concepts of infinity. The numbers, which order the natural world I see around me, also ordered the world in which my ammonite was alive and swimming. It is powerful evidence of the connection between all things – powerful evidence too of just how fragile and fleeting it all is.

Around ninety-nine per cent of all the species that ever lived are now extinct and only a very small fraction are preserved as fossils; an even smaller fraction are ever actually found. And at Mary Anning's shop, you can get all this for just £2.50.

THE FINAL
FRONTIER

Derry Brabbs
on Hadrian's Wall

My FIRST ENCOUNTER WITH Hadrian's Wall was in 1984, while doing the photography for *Wainwright on the Pennine Way* – the second of seven books I illustrated for the legendary Alfred Wainwright. I was already aware of the wall's existence but my vision of it, like so many others, was shaped solely by viewing other people's published images. I had little idea of just how awesome the three-dimensional version would be.

It was a spine-tingling and somewhat humbling experience to stand alone on one of the wall's highest vantage points, touching blocks of stone that were originally slotted into place by soldiers from the Roman legions of York, Chester or Caerleon. The wall, which was started in AD 122 upon the orders of Emperor Hadrian, cleverly utilized the island's narrowest part, extending for some seventy-three miles across the Tyne–Solway isthmus between Carlisle and Newcastle. Nowadays, we take so much for granted and rely on technology for even the most basic tasks. It is easy to forget just how much of our built heritage was accomplished solely through manual labour – including arguably the most important extant monument from the Roman Empire.

Sadly, prolonged stretches at either end of the wall have completely disappeared. In fact, the solid walls of many local churches, farms and manor houses reveal just how much of it was used as a free source of ready-dressed building stone. But there is still much to excite a landscape photographer. The wall can be seen at its spectacular best along the central section between Walltown Crags and Housesteads Fort, where it dips and soars for several miles over the undulations of the Whin Sill ridge. Antisocial early mornings and late nights await those anxious to capitalize on the warm tones and low-angled light of sunrise and sunset – natural attributes that are particularly essential when attempting to highlight the character, contours and definition of the wall.

I have now lost count of the times I have made the two-hour journey up to the wall in pitch blackness – spurred on by the forecast of a brilliant sunrise – only to have those expectations dashed by banks of low cloud or mist. The thought that I might have this slice of history to myself for just a few moments, however, makes it a chance worth taking. For in daylight hours, the only battles this great wall now sees are the ones generated by the increasing amount of pedestrian traffic – especially since the Hadrian's Wall Path National Trail was formally opened in 2003.

Few of those who now tramp along its more clearly defined sections will ever know that it is because of John Clayton (1792–1890) that they can still do so. Clayton is justifiably lauded as being the saviour of Hadrian's Wall. He was appalled at the way in which landowners showed scant regard for the wall's historical value by persistently plundering its stone. In the absence of any conservation or protection bodies – the concept of 'heritage' was restricted to an enlightened minority at that time – he began buying farms and other properties whenever they came up for sale. His labourers were then tasked with the job of clearing and rebuilding long sections of the wall on his newly acquired property. It is only because of this wonderfully altruistic act that this historical masterpiece is there for photographers and tourists alike to enjoy. Without John Clayton, Hadrian's Wall would be nothing more than a good story and a few shards of pottery lying buried under the earth.

RUTLAND HOW I LOVE THEE

Julia Bradbury
on a heart-shaped county

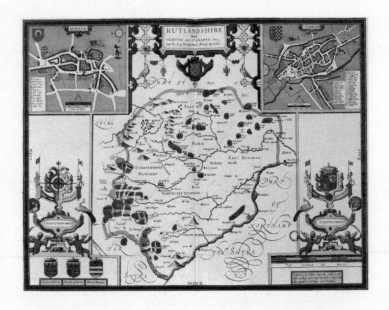

'PLUCK' IS A GREAT word. The people of Rutland have pluck and it is something I've always admired. I have had occasion to read some bird books recently (some of my *Countryfile* assignments have involved ornithology), and I chanced upon Rory McGrath's *Bearded Tit*. This is what he has to say about Rutland: 'For a long time it was subsumed into Leicestershire but the plucky Rutlanders had agitated for it to be restored to its former glory. So now it is Rutland again, with the pretty town of Oakham as its capital; a beacon of hope for a rapidly disappearing Britain.' How wonderful – welcome to a Beacon of Hope.

Whether the county is named after a wealthy landowner (Rota), or was christened Rutland because of its rich red soil is a matter of some debate, but there is no question about its size; the heart-shaped area covers 150 square miles and measures sixteen miles across its widest point east to west. It lies almost in the centre of England. The underlying rock, the most valuable of which is the deliciously named Oolite, dates back to Jurassic and Pleistocene times. Many of the houses across the county are built out of Oolite. I am lucky enough to have grown up in one of those, so the heart shape of Rutland is in my heart.

You cannot talk about Rutland and not mention the Rutland Water. The hamlets of Nether Hambleton and Middle Hambleton were sacrificed in the 1970s to make way for this stretch of water, which has now become an integral part of life here. Sailing, fishing and cruising on the *Rutland Belle* are all common place. Cycling and eating your way around the reservoir are easy to do. Beer festivals, horse trials, endurance races and, let us not forget, walking, are all here for the taking. And the birdwatchers would never forgive me if I didn't encourage you to pick up the binos at the Rutland Osprey Project. Local hero Tim Appleton has helped reintroduce these rare birds that, until now, haven't been in attendance in our skies since 1840.

Whatever your interests, I am sure you can find a little bit of what you're looking for in Rutland. The plucky Rutlanders have not adopted the motto *Multum in Parvo* – 'Much in little' for nothing. In this case small really is beautiful.

IN HIGH PLACES

Melvyn Bragg
on Skiddaw Fell

As you come into Cumbria from the north, which the Picts and Scots did in force of arms for almost 2,000 years, the first big mountain you see across the Solway Plain is Skiddaw. It rises to the south, widespread and large, its bare hide like that of a giant Jurassic beast slumbering.

When the Norsemen came in the ninth century, they brought the word 'fell' for the high hills, along with thousands of other words which are still in use, though less frequently now, in that fortress part of England.

It was to Skiddaw, for those of us who lived on the plain in more Christian times, that you 'lifted up your eyes'. It had something of the holy mountain about it, a trace memory of the age in which high places were held in awe, seeming mysterious and majestic, the lairs of fearful spirits.

It was a stiff bike ride to get there from my own town, Wigton, upwards of twenty miles, and even my young legs would get too tired to get right to the summit in the early days. The more measured years of youth-hostelling allowed time for the full hike, and after that it became just part of a long day's trawl across the northern Fells.

With friends I've hauled an absurdly inappropriate picnic up the south side (there is a remarkable account of a wagon train of a picnic ascending Skiddaw in the early nineteenth century). With my son I've gone the long way, from our cottage – up beside Dash Falls, along the valley to Half Way House, through sweet bleak country, then a sharp turn west to the top.

Coleridge brooded daily on Skiddaw from his house near Keswick. He appreciated, as I have done over forty years, the marvel of change. Cloud-capped, totally hidden, half seen, snow-layered, tonsured with a cloud below, wisps and veils of cloud lingering in the gulleys, driven by rain and hail, and on some days so cleanly cut out and brimming with the quiet mix of green and brown and grey that the fell appears almost unreal, pasted on to the bare blue sky.

There are days when the sun shines through holes in the clouds in shafts, once known as 'stairways to heaven'. Then there is the night-time mass. And in moonlight, the dense black shape is silhouetted against the thinner black of the sky.

The underlying rock is grey slate. There is in Keswick Museum a primitive musical instrument, an enormous xylophone made entirely from Skiddaw slates, each of which gives off a different note. It was famous in its day and shipped down to London to be performed upon in the presence of Queen Victoria.

So inside Skiddaw Fell there is music, on it there is weather which in a single day can rage through the seasons, and from its summit is a view that reaches into Scotland, across to the Pennines, deep into the Lake District, peak after peak, and below you the only 'lake' so named in Cumbria: Bassenthwaite.

Once, shivering behind the cairn on the summit, sipping tea in a wild and furious west wind, I saw a hawk and it appeared static. Self-suspended in the gale force, shivering in the total pleasure in being alive, then, there.

RURAL
DEVELOPMENT

Jo Brand
on a country childhood

I GREW UP IN the garden of England, the Weald of Kent, surrounded by hopfields, beech woods, animals, birds and a general sense of peace and beauty. Being the middle girl of two brothers however, I tended to be involved in the constant struggle of sibling competition with my brothers. Our battles were invariably fought in a number of rural arenas including the woods, fields and rivers of our childhood.

We disturbed wasps nests. On one occasion, I ran one way and my brothers the other, and they ended up with all the stings. I was triumphant.

On another occasion, we swung out on a dodgy piece of rope over a small stream. They cleared it, I didn't, and I ended up sitting on my arse in the stream-bed with their gleeful, smug laughter ringing in my ears, a sound that always spurred me on to greater acts of revenge.

We held races, climbing competitions, fights with pieces of wood, Chinese-burn contests and dared each other to more and more stupid activities.

One day they both pushed a gate I was sitting on, causing me to fly backwards off it, ripping my arm on barbed wire as I fell. The huge importance of courage in the face of injury overtook the supreme pain and I trod a dignified path back home, holding the contents of my arm in without shedding a tear until my crowing brothers were out of sight.

But it wasn't always a battlefield in our rural idyll. Occasionally we managed to cooperate against the enemy. For a year or so, my dad's rented seven-acre field was home to three donkeys – a mother and two sons – and on discovering that if you touch the top of a donkey's tail it goes absolutely bonkers, we invited a series of children from school for a ride, sat them on, touched the top of the tail, and let the donkey do its worst.

Eventually the three donkeys conspired to get themselves removed by eating a thousand baby-Christmas trees lovingly planted by my dad, and they were shunted off to pastures new.

But it is these memories that shine brightest in the fragmented store of my childhood recollections. Sunlit days with nothing better to do than throw leaves at each other, or clear blue wintry days sledging down the field on an improvised vehicle to certain injury at the bottom. I'm sure Wordsworth put it so much better than I could in *The Prelude*, but a country childhood sits inside you, always filling you with a feeling of well-being. I could not imagine I would have had such a happy beginning had I spent my formative years in the Smoke.

THE URBAN VILLAGE

Vincent Cable
on summer fêtes

To an outsider, our big cities, suburbs and towns can represent a characterless urban sprawl. If there is any subdivision, it is marked by a train station or a shopping centre or the boundaries of a council ward (which will be unknown to everyone except the councillors). Yet there is often a vibrant social and civic life, and a strong sense of local identity, as clearly defined as those of a traditional village with its pub, cricket pitch and parish church.

I discovered, when I came to represent a stretch of suburban south-west London called Twickenham, just how important these urban villages can be. What the boundary commissioners called 'Twickenham' comprises several such villages: Hampton, Hampton Hill and Hampton Wick, Teddington, Whitton, St Margarets, as well as Twickenham itself. They are loosely linked to council wards and parishes and give their names to Scout troops, schools and sectors of the local property market. That is unremarkable. What is more remarkable is that these villages function in an urban setting much like traditional villages, where people have a real sense of belonging and commitment.

The centrepiece of village life is the annual fair, where the charities and local traders have their stalls; brass bands play; beautiful babies compete for rosettes, likewise dogs; children's faces are painted; the bars do record business; celebrities play cricket; and dignitaries dress up and parade, trying to impersonate Her Majesty's wave. The enemy, of course, is British rain. Several of the villages in my patch have a winter street fair as well, with Father Christmas instead of the carnival queen and punch instead of Pimm's.

Dozens of people devote months of work to these events, which are always thronged.

The energy behind the organization of the village fairs also sustains a thriving civic culture. I continue to be amazed at the proliferation of drama groups, choirs and orchestras; the school, Scout and church fund-raising dos; the ex-servicemen's groups, model-train clubs and allotment associations; the boys' (and increasingly, girls') and adult football and rugby teams which fill all available local parkland on a Sunday morning. The notion that 'there is no such thing as society' is continually contradicted.

The urban village is, however, more than just a hive of social activity. It provides a sense of identity, and place, in an otherwise anonymous urban environment. Many of these urban villages were once rural villages sucked into expanding cities. In the case of my part of London, the arrival of trains and trams in the late nineteenth century transformed villages into suburbs. The parish church and graveyard provide that longer historical context. But the village is not just a set of historical monuments; it has re-emerged as a living urban community.

THE VIEW FROM THE URALS

Adrian Chiles
on the Clent Hills

THE HOUSE I WAS raised in, where my parents still live, is at the foot of the Clent Hills in Hagley, which is either in Worcestershire or the West Midlands, nobody seems quite sure. If you're posh you say Worcestershire; if you want to disguise your impeccable middle-class credentials – as I do – you say West Midlands.

I looked up at the Clent Hills every time I opened my curtains in the morning. I didn't think much about them, though – they were just a geographical feature I was occasionally forced to march up at the weekend, especially if we had visitors staying who needed to be shown something.

When I was a teenager there was a pub in Clent which could be persuaded to serve under-eighteens intoxicating liquor, so I was to be found there most weekends, lolling around in the grass of the lower slopes, trying to pretend I enjoyed Old Roger or whatever super-strong real ale we'd managed to get our lips round.

It wasn't until I was well into adulthood that I fell in love with Clent properly. I was in my late twenties and I'd taken up running. I ran to the very top one autumn evening and, looking to the west, suddenly felt completely sure that there is no better view anywhere in the world.

Worcestershire, the Malvern Hills, market towns dotted here and there and, possibly, mid-Wales dimly visible in the distance: Central England in all its ancient magnificence.

But it's better than that, because if you look east, there's the uncompromising, grey urban sprawl of Birmingham and the Black Country squatting there before you. I can't say it's beautiful, but it's dramatic; it has balls. And, what's more, it throws the bucolic beauty of the view to the west into sharper, heart-stopping focus.

I'm occasionally arrested by a vision of what it must have been like to stand up there fifty years ago, surveying the country's industrial heartland. Back in the day, when people actually made things, that view to the east must have pulsated, oozed and smoked with quite satanic fervour. To the west, those greens and browns must have looked, by contrast, so much more pure and heavenly.

One more thing about the view to the east over Birmingham: when the wind blows from there, it's cold. Really, really cold. That's because, I've always been told, the next highest point in that direction is in the Ural mountains in Russia. I've half-checked this fact and it seems plausible, but I've never verified it for sure because I so want it to be true. I have this image of a couple of Cossacks out for a walk up those Urals. One takes a big swig of vodka out of a bottle, burps, and passes it to his mate saying, 'You know, Boris, on a clear day you can see Clent from here.' Boris nods, impressed.

WHAT A WASTE

Eric Clapton
on Newlands Corner

As a young boy growing up in the 1950s, country life was pretty much all I knew. My family lived in Ripley, Surrey, right on the edge of the village green and, as a result, my pursuits were simple, healthy and modest – mainly consisting of games of Cowboys and Indians in the nearby woods. Visits to other villages and towns were few and far between. And a trip to Guildford, which was only about six miles away, was a special event.

In the summer, however, there were often village junkets to the seaside. The British Legion or one of the pubs on the high street would usually organize these excursions, ferrying us down in ancient charabancs to places like Bognor, Brighton or Littlehampton. And they were always memorable – mainly for the humorous misfortunes of people getting lost or left behind, breakdowns miles from anywhere and incredible sing-songs there, with beer-fuelled ones on the way back. I loved the way we would amble through the strange new countryside at twenty miles per hour, everyone buzzing with excitement. And I loved being caught up in the thrill of leaving the village behind, heading into the unknown.

For me, the sight of unfamiliar landscape was like a drug. I would look forward to it all through the winter, and it spawned something in me which has never died – a compulsion to travel. Several landmarks were burnt into my memory back then: Bury Hill, a place so steep we usually had to get out and push the coach; Newlands Corner, which was the first sign of the mystical lands beyond the borders of Ripley; and the sight and smell of the sea as we approached the coast, coupled with the mad scramble to the front of the coach and the fight to be the first to scream, 'I can see the sea.'

In hindsight, the value of these sights and sounds has grown immeasurably over the years. None more so than Newlands Corner, an area about six hundred feet high, which can be seen from the Dorking Road just outside Guildford. In my twenties, when I set up home near the village of Cranleigh, it marked the final glorious five miles of my journey home. And there is nothing better than leaving the suburbs of the town to climb gradually up the winding road until you reach the top of the hill. As you come over the crest, you are treated to one of the most beautiful sights known to man – or this man, anyway.

I must have looked at this gorgeous panorama thousands and thousands of times. But it still causes me to gasp and hold my breath. It's not particularly grand – the scale of the Surrey Hills is quite small – but the proportions are absolutely perfect. A patchwork of fields and woodland is laid carefully over the gently undulating North Downs in such an exquisite design that it's always a massive temptation to stop the car, get out and let the healing take place. It's also quite a shock to contemplate just how many little homesteads and farms are neatly tucked into the landscape, revealing just how well man and nature can work together. If only man could always blend in so successfully.

It's a sad thing, then, for me to consider that in my lifetime I will have watched this amazing place evolve into a massive rubbish dump. For the last decade, a mountain of waste has been quietly growing out of the landscape. The site itself has been a sandpit for as long as I can remember, but gradually it has morphed into something a little more ominous. Its purpose is to try to get rid of things that don't particularly want to go away: plastic in all its different forms – bags, bottles and so on.

At present, the authorities are doing their best to make sense of it all, researching the possibility of using the methane from the waste to fuel the trucks that carry it in such vast quantities. But at the rate it's growing, it will soon be as high as the hill across the valley – my Newlands Corner. Time – and space – is running out.

Complaining is my God-given birthright. I love it, and am very good at it. It is, however, usually directed towards someone I know will sympathize with my argument, and is therefore 'safe'. In this case, I'm sure it's already too late. I have watched this problem developing over the past few years and have done absolutely nothing about it. I have complained, but only to my wife, who patiently hears me out – then makes me a cup of tea. My complaining has done nothing other than reveal the extent of my social incompetence and irresponsibility. I am, I admit, ashamed of myself. I fear I have witnessed the passing of something my children and grandchildren will, in all probability, never see – the beauty of Newlands Corner.

BACK ON DRY LAND

Sue Clifford
on limestone

KNEE-DEEP IN A ford, fingers under the stones searching out bullheads; leaping across dry stones where a river should be flowing or standing deep in a dripping cavern singing with glistening towers – it occurs to me that I learnt about happiness and freedom, beauty and the land, from limestone.

My parents loved Derbyshire and whenever time allowed, we were up on the moors or deep in the dales. Already I was being tutored in contrasts – exposed sycamore-embraced farms, valleys and quarries defining each other, the Dark Peak with its summer holiday cotton grass or winter cold edges of millstone grit; the White Peak with its patterns of dry-stone walls and dew ponds. That I should spend my life championing local distinctiveness seems, in retrospect, inevitable.

Limestone is variegated. The pyramid of Thorpe Cloud guards Dovedale – the name alone entices me – and I am still impressed by Peter's Stone, a coral-reef knoll as big as a church between Wardlow and Litton. It stands surrounded by cropped grass, framed in a streamless cliffed valley. Three hundred and fifty million years ago, fish flew by in a warm sea that was nurturing what we know as carboniferous limestone. This Pennine reef limestone is cemented so tight with fossils and remains that the water finds it hard to penetrate.

It is always a pleasure to bump into fossils: the so-called 'Purbeck marbles' are full of shells, and form dark pillars and carvings inside many a church. On polished walls and floors such as those of London's Festival Hall, you can find the confused patterns of Hopton Wood crinoidal limestone from Derbyshire. And on the beach at Holy Island in Northumberland, you can pick up St Cuthbert's Beads, the little coins of crinoid stems.

Great underground systems are found in the Mendips in Somerset, and in Derbyshire and Yorkshire. Here too are gorges – enormous at Cheddar and Matlock Bath, narrow but awesome at Gaping Ghyll. Perhaps they are great collapsed caverns, their ice-melt streams shrunken now to little misfits or completely gone, leaving, for example, the high, dry waterfall at Malham Cove. The higher lands are dotted with swallets, sinkholes and waterfalls into netherworlds. Water plays hide and seek, reappearing as risings, springs and boilings in rivers. And in between there is a world of dissolving and dripping, stalactites and stalagmites, calciferous creativity to be chanced upon by cavers, or worn down by the eyes of tourists.

For all the limestones the common thread on the surface is the dry valley, but they do vary. The Mendips fold gently, the Jurassic oolites of the Cotswolds roll. In deep Pennine valleys you can walk along sections of dry riverbeds, as in Lathkill Dale or the Manifold. The situation of villages and farms shows where water is (or was), and in the White Peak of Derbyshire, thanks for water are still given at the well-dressing ceremonies in the high villages.

Our buildings speak most when they tell local stories of the rock beneath. In Portland and Purbeck in Dorset, the variety of limestone beds is used in different ways – local masons and wallers have left a legacy of buildings, roofs and field walls of some substance. And across the country quarries abound. You can see where the houses and walls come from along the 'limestone belt' from Portland to Bath, through the Cotswolds, Northamptonshire, Huntingdonshire, Rutland and Lincolnshire.

From mines at nearby Box, Bath stone helps give Bath its honey colour. Buxton, greyer, is wrought of limestone from down the road. But the demand for cement, road stone and aggregate for roads, runways, car parks, harbours and concrete means the Sandford and Dulcote Hills in the Mendips are set to halve in size, demeaning the place and the stone. This makes all the more poignant W. H. Auden's vision from 'In Praise of Limestone':

> *. . . but when I try to imagine a faultless love*
> *Or the life to come, what I hear is the murmur*
> *Of underground streams, what I see is a limestone*
> *landscape.*

RHYME AND REASON

Wendy Cope
on water meadows

When I first moved to Winchester in 1994 and began walking in the water meadows several times a week, I felt as if I had come home to an England I had always loved. That it felt like a homecoming made no sense because I had lived in the London suburbs during my childhood and for most of my life. Perhaps what I came home to was a vision of the perfect English landscape, glimpsed in films and on rural excursions. Here, right on my doorstep, was a landscape that lived up to the vision.

The water meadows are on the southern edge of Winchester, three minutes from the street where I live and ten minutes from the high street. There's a path through them that runs between two waterways: a millstream known as Logie and the much wider river Itchen. On the first part of the walk, going south, there are fields and trees on the far side of each waterway, and in the distance is St Catherine's Hill. Everything as far as the eye can see belongs to Winchester College, but the path is open to the public and its dogs.

At some point in the 1980s there was a plan to run the M3 through the water meadows. The headmaster of Winchester and some of his staff attended the public inquiry and made their presence felt by humming. It sounds to me like a risky strategy for schoolmasters – they would have been in trouble if their pupils had borrowed the idea in school. But, eventually, the plan was altered. Despite the best efforts of protesters, the motorway cuts through nearby Twyford Down instead.

If I listen out for it, I can hear some traffic noise on my walks, except when it is drowned by the sound from a culvert or a weir. I also hear birdsong, and, now and then, the humming wings of flying swans. And I often stop to watch the water birds – coots, moorhens, dippers and ducks – going about their business.

The poet John Keats stayed in Winchester for six weeks in 1819. In a letter to his brother he described his daily walk, which took him past the cathedral and along College Street, where – although he wasn't aware of it – he passed the house where Jane Austen had died two years earlier. Then he followed the path through the water meadows all the way to the ancient almshouse, the Hospital of St Cross, which is still there today. He told a correspondent that 'there are the most beautiful streams I ever saw, full of trout'. They are still beautiful and you can still see trout in the Itchen.

On his walk on 19 September, Keats was so struck by the beauty of the season and the 'temperate sharpness' of the air that he 'composed upon it'. The result was his ode 'To Autumn'. It was his last great poem. Already ill, he died seventeen months later, aged twenty-five. It moves me to know that my regular walk is much the same as his, and to reflect on my good fortune in having had so many years to enjoy it.

ALL A BROAD

Nicholas Crane
on the Broads

Hanging above the grocery shelves in Ludham Bridge Stores is a very strange map. Tubers of sea protrude far inland from a coastline which bears no resemblance to modern topography. Lean over the home-made apple pies and you realize that this is a map of the Great Estuary, the vast tidal waterway which evolved over two thousand years into England's largest protected wetland: sixty-three shallow lakes and 122 miles of lock-free rivers, spanning two counties and collectively known as the Broads. This secretive water garden is as English as chalk grassland and sooty gritstone, but it is facing change.

Back in the days when Boadicea and her Iceni tribe controlled the Great Estuary, this was a trading haven to rival the Thames. The Iceni capital prospered on one of the estuary's tendrils and the region's soils were intensively farmed for grain and sheep. Where yachts tack today between the channel markers on Breydon Water, freight barges scudded over a vast inland sea whose five-mile mouth was defended by the Romans with a pair of gigantic forts. It must have been an extraordinary spectacle; teeming with marine life, its mouth opening on to a glittering inland sea fed by innumerable creeks and rivers.

I grew up close to the Great Estuary's tributaries. Every morning I'd cycle to school over the river Yare and I remember scrambling through the brambles in the Roman town of Venta Icenorum, long before it was cleared for visitors. At weekends we canoed on the Bure or capsized the family dinghy on Hickling Broad. And where I learned to row a coxed-four on Whitlingham Marsh, the towering steel hulls of freighters used to thud upstream towards Norwich, loaded with Baltic timber. Thirty miles from the sea, they looked utterly lost.

The Great Estuary was an environmental accident waiting to happen. After the Romans went home, sea levels fell relative to the land, and the mouth of the estuary silted up. Vast bogs and marshes formed where boats once sailed. It's a bit unclear when the Broads were formed, but for around four hundred years, through the Middle Ages, some nine hundred million cubic feet of peat were excavated from the region for domestic fuel and for industrial processes such as salt-making. A series of catastrophic inundations and rising sea levels gradually flooded the peat diggings.

Today, this wetland moves me way beyond the reckonings of an amphibious boyhood. Every time I haul the mainsail, I know that the wind will carry our boat into a place where water and land are in a state of precarious balance. This is England's most impermanent landscape, preserved by pumps and dykes, which cannot keep pace with the rising waters. Science warns that accelerated sea-level rise, the increased likelihood of North Sea surges and violent storms look set to flood many of the acres reclaimed over the last two thousand years. Natural England has estimated that six villages and twenty-five square miles of Norfolk could be lost to the sea within a century. The Broads will become saline. Ecosystems will change. East Norfolk is on the front line of climate change.

So I no longer take for granted the river's lovely windings past How Hill, or the sight of a wherry heeling by flint-knapped St Benet's. Sail quietly, and you can see kingfishers, marsh harriers and herons attending the banks in their grey tailcoats. Otters have returned, and there is an alder carr where owls hunt at dusk. On the Broads, there is always the unexpected: a few weeks ago, moored for the night in the lee of a spectral windmill, I went out on deck to silence a slapping halyard, and on tying it back, the sound of a lonely bittern and a faraway church could be heard playing a wetland duet across the starlit flats.

REBUILDING THE PAST

Dan Cruickshank
on the Euston Arch

My ICON OF ENGLAND is a building that does not currently exist but that lives in the memory and imagination and that could, if we want it to, yet rise from the grave.

Demolished in early 1962 after a short, sharp campaign to save it, the Euston Arch was a London landmark for over 120 years. It was the first major monument of the epoch-making railway age, the centrepiece of Euston Station, which when it opened in 1837 was the first main-line railway terminus built in any capital city in the world. The arch, completed in May of the following year, was the architectural wonder of its time. It was one of the finest Greek-revival buildings in the world – a memorial to the Golden Age of antiquity – yet at the same time a symbol of modernity, of the dawn of a new era of communication and transport. It was also the gate to and from the north, through which flowed the wealth of the land.

The arch, designed by Philip Hardwick, was the largest Greek Doric propylaeum, or gateway, ever built. Standing over seventy feet high, it was a sublime, elemental construction, particularly in its latter years when the granite-hard Bramley Fall gritstone with which it was faced had acquired a silky black patina of soot deposits from steam engines and coal fires.

While the arch was a meticulous copy of much-admired historic prototypes – notably the Propylaeum of c. 450 BC, which led to the top of the Acropolis in Athens – it was modern in terms of its ingenious and pioneering construction. Although it appeared to be built of traditional masonry, it incorporated much iron. Hardwick wanted to minimize construction costs by reducing the weight of the arch and the quantity of expensive materials employed, so the Bramley Fall gritstone (4,420 tons of it, delivered by rail from Yorkshire) was used to clad a robust iron-and-brick inner structure. For example, each column 'drum' was not solid but hollow, being composed of four slabs fixed together with metal clamps and braces.

The failure to save the arch in late 1961 was a bitter and public defeat for the forces of civilization and culture – headed by Sir John Betjeman and the Victorian Society – and a victory for the penny-pinching forces of crude modernization headed by British Railways, aided and abetted by the British government. But the loss of the Euston arch – which appalled the British public – helped to kick-start the conservation movement. Never again it was felt should such a gross act of barbarism be committed in the public's name, yet against the public's wishes. And so the sacrifice of the Euston arch helped save the station buildings at St Pancras and King's Cross, because it was clear to both British Railways and to politicians that such cavalier and brutish conduct could not be repeated.

Public fury was partly due to the fact that most people had assumed that the arch was safe and its future guaranteed. In 1937-8, when the London Midland and Scottish Railway first announced its intention to rebuild Euston Station, the nascent Georgian Group persuaded it to do the decent thing and re-site the arch on the Euston Road. The Second World War put a stop to redevelopment of the station, but when it was discussed again in the late 1950s it was generally assumed that the arch was to be saved. Only in 1960 did it emerge that British Railways and the British Transport Commission wanted to renege on their earlier assurances and save time and money by simply demolishing rather than carefully dismantling and reconstructing the monument. Their betrayal seemed all the more bitter when the Victorian Society demonstrated that moving the arch on rails was technically possible and reasonably cheap.

The final decision on the future of the arch lay with the government and the Prime Minister, Harold Macmillan. Despite intense lobbying from informed individuals and conservation organizations, the government declined to make the British Transport Commission stand by its promise and refused to provide money to move the arch, rejecting advice from the Victorian Society urging that time was pressing. And so, to the intense shock and stunned disbelief of many, demolition took place.

Frank Valori, the man employed by British Railways to demolish the arch, implied soon after destruction that, on his own initiative, he had numbered the stones, dismantled them carefully and stored them. Sadly, this was not true. In the early 1990s two short films about the Euston Arch and its destruction were made for BBC2 and they revealed the arch's true fate. Demolition was speedy and brutal, with the stones being broken and much damaged as the arch was speedily cleared away. Some of the stones were used by Valori in the construction of his own house – Paradise Villa in Bromley, Kent – although around sixty per cent of them were used to level and 'armour' the bed of the Prescott

Channel, off the River Lea at Three Mills in Bow, East London. This site was investigated in 1994: one stone slab – part of one of the arch's column drums – was lifted and is now stored in the garden of a house in Stockwell. Following the discovery of the site of the stones the Euston Arch Trust (EAT) was set up to campaign for the reconstruction of the arch – using as many original stones as possible – at or near Euston Station.

Since 1994 much has happened. The currently proposed redevelopment of the 1960s Euston Station provides a logical opportunity for the reconstruction of the arch at Euston. The location of the Olympic site near Three Mills in Bow has meant the construction of a large new lock on the Prescott Channel and dredging works at and around the location of the stones. These have been conducted with great sensitivity by British Waterways, and led in 2009, with the assistance of EAT, to the location of many more stones and the lifting of twenty-five, including part of a capital of one of the piers, carved entablature and another slab forming part of a column drum.

The issues raised by the campaign to rebuild the arch are complex. A lost building can be rebuilt, but can its spirit be re-created? It is the view of EAT – and its supporters, including English Heritage and the Georgian Group, that by using a large number of original stones, as part of a reconstruction undertaken with conviction and honest intent, the new arch would be more than a shallow pastiche. It would be an act of heroic repair, demonstrating that it is possible to right a great wrong and bring beauty back from a watery grave. If nothing else, EAT's campaign provokes a profound debate about the nature and role of conservation and the philosophy of repair.

Another debate has to do with the function a reconstructed arch would fulfil if built as an entrance to a redeveloped Euston Station. Should it be made to serve as a practical public building, or should it be simply a symbol?

One thing, however, is clear – now is the arch's golden chance. Euston Station is scheduled to be redeveloped and the splendid renaissance of neighbouring St Pancras and King's Cross stations has whetted the public's appetite for Victorian railway architecture and history, and demonstrates how the old and the new can work together in a most thrilling and creative manner. Reconstruction of the arch would cause delight and wonder around the world, and give a rebuilt Euston character and distinction. For, in the most powerful way possible, it would demonstrate that lost beauty can live again.

FROM THE TRENCHES

General Sir Richard Dannatt
on Breckland

TO THOSE WHO LIVE in Norfolk, it is known as the 'battle area'. To many soldiers, it is remembered as a very sandy training area, characterized by collapsing trench walls. But Stanford Training Area, located to the north of Thetford, is also the last surviving major piece of English Breckland.

The estate lies in the heart of the Brecks, a place characterized by heathland. This important natural habitat consists of an intimate mosaic of chalk and acid grassland situated in an area with a semi-continental climate – hotter summers, colder winters and considerably less-than-average annual rainfall. Consequently, much of the flora and fauna are unique to the area.

There is a diverse range of over six hundred flowering plants, thirty-two species of butterfly, over four hundred species of moth, and nearly thirty species of mammal (the most prolific being the rabbit). The area also contains one of the most significant bat hibernaculums in the county – bats use the heathland as a hunting ground. And it has witnessed the resurgence of the stone curlew which, while not exclusively restricted to heathland, seems to thrive on the Stanford heath – there are currently twenty-one pairs nesting there. On exercise a few years ago, one of my soldiers – a resident of Middlesbrough – turned to me in amazement. 'Sir, it's like a game park here!'

Of course, this beautiful habitat hasn't always belonged to us. And it hasn't always been beautiful. In 1942, 40,500 hectares were requisitioned to provide a wartime training facility. After the war, the land was purchased from private investors and the then Forestry Commission. It has remained a training area ever since and now comprises a little over 8,330 hectares of freehold land. Military ownership has not protected it from degradation caused by intensive agricultural development – of the 32,000 hectares of heath in the 1930s, only 7,000 hectares remained in 1980, and two thirds of this was on the training area. In 1987 we decided to bring back some of the lost heathland, and by the year 2000 almost 634 hectares had been recreated and regenerated from clear-fell, arable and from introducing grazing. Almost three-quarters of the estate is now designated as a Site of Special Scientific Interest.

Stanford remains one of the busiest training areas in the UK, with up to 100,000 soldiers training on the area in any one year. But conservation is never far from our thoughts. A more formal management approach enables us to provide training while safeguarding and enhancing the environment and the interests of our stakeholders. Already we have initiated the clearance of ponds for the great crested newts and made improvements to the nesting plots for the stone curlews. An area that can benefit both those about to deploy on operations and our nation's wildlife, this is an area that will always be worth protecting.

BESIDE THE SEASIDE

Jonathan Dimbleby
on the beach at West Wittering

I FIRST WENT TO West Wittering more than fifty years ago. I was a small child cramped in the back of a Morris Minor estate (or 'shooting brake' as they were then known). We drove past Chichester Cathedral, down an endless leafy Sussex lane, past cows in fields and a scatter of cottages until suddenly we were there, jolting across the turf to park up close to a tamarisk hedge which bordered speargrass and mountainous sand dunes that concealed our view of the sea. But we could smell the brine and hear the hiss of the surf.

We would race through a gap in the hedge to our beach hut. Sand was always piled up against the door, blown up by the westerlies that drove in across the Solent. Some of the finer grains would have infiltrated the hut itself, depositing a light sprinkling of yellowish dust on the Primus stove, a huddle of worn deckchairs, the black inner tube of a car tyre (the best rubber ring ever), and a detritus of buckets, spades and rubber balls.

When the tide was in, we braved the breakers and when it was out, we built sandcastles and paddled in the lagoons looking for crabs and sea urchins. Such simple pleasures. At the end of the day we ate sand-flecked jam sandwiches and drank Bovril before piling back into the car, scratching the salt and sand out of our hair and so exhausted that we were invariably asleep long before Chichester Cathedral came into view again from the opposite direction.

The wonder of West Wittering is that it has hardly changed in half a century. No amusement parks and no stalls selling useless trinkets. There is now a toll booth (five pounds per car), a modest café and a windsurfing club. But the huts are still there, their soft blues and greens and browns faded by salt winds and age. The beach (which still seems to stretch towards eternity in either direction) is busier but not crowded. Children still skip in and out of the water, defying the waves, or construct elaborate castles in the sand. They still play cricket and volleyball. And they still fly kites, though these are now far larger and more elaborate, threatening to lift even big brothers all the way across to the Isle of Wight. Elderly couples still stroll along the water's edge with overweight Labrador dogs. There is no litter and no music.

There are differences, of course. Most notably, the wooden breakwaters which used to stride out into the sea, towering over my head, have all but disappeared under the sand. And the dunes where we used to hide are sadly diminished. However, the West Wittering Estate (which bought the 250-hectare estate in 1952 for what today seems to be a peppercorn £21,000, to save it from becoming a leisure centre) is making valiant efforts to stabilize and restore this precious heritage, fencing off and reseeding the most vulnerable areas.

The view to seaward has changed as well. Half a century ago, when Britain had yet to escape wartime austerity, the Solent was virtually deserted, except for an occasional liner; I once saw the *Queen Elizabeth* (two funnels to the *Queen Mary's* three) steaming out from Southampton. Now this weekend waterway is strewn with expensive yachts and glossy speedboats. But they are merely the backdrop to a very English art form that has yet to perish: a simple afternoon at the seaside.

A PASSION FOR MEAT

Wilfred Emmanuel-Jones
on family butchers

FOR ME, ONE OF the joys of visiting a rural town is seeking out the local family butcher. You can always tell the good ones, as on Saturday mornings there's a queue of people snaking out of the door and around the corner. What grieves me is that this sight is increasingly becoming a rarity, yet another casualty of the lure of out-of-town shopping. We now have to work harder to find these tradesmen, but find them we must, and support them by using them. The traditional butcher is an exceptional person. Probably unbeknown to him, it is one such person who opened my eyes to the sheer art of butchery. Philip Warren of Warren's butchers in Launceston, Cornwall had a huge impact on me when I first met him and he helped me to decide to produce beef cattle, for what he doesn't know about beef really isn't worth knowing. From that early meeting I made my decision to farm Ruby Reds, a beautiful and delicious breed indigenous to the West Country. Philip comes up to my farm in person to take a look at the animals and decide which ones are ready for him. He selects his animals for slaughter, following which they go to his shop for hanging to develop the flavour. It is this personal attention to detail that sets the master butcher apart.

Philip's passion for meat, like that of every master butcher, is evident in his shop window. Every cut of meat is equal in his eyes and is displayed with pride, whether it's a prime sirloin steak or rib of beef, or a pig's trotter. The window makes a feature of the names of the farmers and farms where the animals were reared. It doesn't come much more traceable than this. A master butcher is to meat what a Master of Wine is to wine. The artistry involved in this profession will be demonstrated most clearly by those working in the rooms at the back of the shop, however. Here you will find the carcasses hanging to mature and an army of butchers hard at work hacking, sawing, boning and preparing cuts of meat that probably only our grandparents would have used on a regular basis. It is local butchers such as these who are keeping these great traditions alive; they are a treasure trove for the interested cook and we should use them for information and guidance and good old-fashioned service. They deserve our support, even if it does mean making an extra journey. The quality of the meat you will buy and the sheer wonderment at visiting such a shop will be reward enough to keep you going back.

READING THE SIGNS

Sebastian Faulks
on pub signs

THE PUB IN THE village where I was born was called the Three Horse Shoes. The sign hung in a timber frame at the top of a white post, the horseshoes making an inverted equilateral triangle, with the brewer's name, Ushers, in capitals underneath. To a child, everything about this sign was intriguing. We lived in horse country, between Newbury and Lambourn, and I was susceptible to the magic of the lucky shoe and number. The word 'Ushers' was also fascinating to me. I pictured men in long black gowns, going about some ancient brewing rite. Then there was the seedy romance of the pub itself. As well as a public and a saloon bar, the Shoes had an off-sales hatch, where an underage errand boy could be sent to fetch back bottles of Courage Light Ale. I couldn't wait to be old enough to go in, to breathe the forbidden air of beer and cool stone flags.

Between the ages of twenty and forty, I spent too much time in pubs. I loved the anonymity, the louche but friendly atmosphere. They were boozers then, which seldom had food, let alone a choice of Thai main courses. You went to drink ale and smoke. In the early 1970s Watneys tried to do away with beer and substitute it with pressurized stuff that tasted of weak tea and soda water. I felt compelled to drink ever more real ale to keep the small brewers alive.

Any journey by car through England for me then was punctuated by the lucky dip of the pub stop. The signs themselves were often a good indicator. Fox and Hounds, Free House, with a jolly hunting scene was worth a look: proper beer and possibly some rudimentary food, such as sausage and mash. Anything with the word Watneys on the sign was out; not just out, in fact, but to be sneered and hooted at. Courage pub signs became uniform, as I remember, and this was disappointing; it gave them a corporate feeling that was the opposite of what individual pubs with their quirky names should exude. Courage was OK, if nothing better was on offer. They had gone the fizzy route with their keg 'JC', but had retained proper bitter and a stronger, soupier brew called Directors. Some people asked for lager. This puzzled me. It was like going to buy a shirt, being offered cotton or linen, but insisting on nylon.

The Marquis of Granby, the Wheatsheaf, the Queen's Head . . . these were usually reliable places. At Grantchester, near Cambridge, where I studied pubs with dedication, there was a Red Lion and a Green Man. One was everything a pub should be – open fire, real beer, dim lights; the other was bright, chilly and sold fizz. I can't remember which way round it was, but the last time I went to the village there was one called the Rupert Brooke. Oh well.

I expect there is a website somewhere which explains who the Marquis of Granby was and why so many pubs are named after him. Perhaps it also explains why all pub signs seem to be constructed in only one way, as described above: the wooden playing card dangling in a frame or, in town, extended from brickwork on a wrought-iron arm. I think this has an effect on the whole country. Whether you are walking in the Lake District or going home from work in Liverpool or Plymouth, you see this same rectangle, swinging free in wind or rain. The pub sign says: you are still in England. Come in here and – however far from home you are, however outlandish our name – you will find the comforts of your local town or village, the same drinks made by the same people, the same rows of spirits behind the bar, the same salty crisps and, to be honest, much the same conversation.

Yet there is something daring and romantic about those names. I don't mean the Hippo and Peignoir, or deliberately silly ones. I mean the Jack of Diamonds or the Hare and Hounds. Perhaps those words, with their evocation of gaming and sports, lured too many good men to their doom. If they had been called the A641 Ring Road Beer House, would anyone have gone there? But who could resist the combination of the exotic and the familiar promised by such places as the Dundas Arms, Mother Black Cap, the Admiral Codrington, the Surprise, the Phoenix, the Rowbarge and the Crooked Billet? They seem to reach down into a folk history that is rich and weird, to something pagan and ritualistic; yet they are as English as the downs from which you first see them swinging in the wind, like hanged men on a gibbet.

People who think of England as a practical country with little flair for the visual would never have imagined that its lanes and roads would be regularly punctuated by what look like cards from a wooden tarot pack – optical extravagances, creakily offering delight, escape and risk. But it is so; and sometimes we hardly see the strangest things by which we are surrounded.

ANOTHER TIME,
ANOTHER PLACE

Bryan Ferry
on Penshaw Monument

PENSHAW MONUMENT IS A half-sized replica of the Temple of Hephaestus in Athens. Built in 1844 at Penshaw, close to Sunderland, it was dedicated to the first Earl of Durham. High on a hill in the middle of an otherwise flat part of the north-east coastal plain, it dominates the surrounding land; and as a young boy growing up in the nearby pit village of Washington, it made a huge impression on me.

My father was born on the side of the hill and farmed there as a young man. He frequently took me to see the view from the top of the hill, which he thought was the best in the world; and there he told me the stories of his youth.

For me, the plain but imposing Doric columns of the monument took on heroic proportions, and seemed to represent a grandeur and sophistication of a better time and a better place. They suggested a certain mystery, something that was missing from my life in that bleak industrial environment. Even though it was essentially a folly, a building without purpose, I was lucky to have such a strong image as an iconic focus for my memories of childhood.

RIDING HIGH

Dick Francis
on the Berkshire Downs

THE MODERN-DAY MOTORIST can travel from Reading to Swindon down the M4 motorway in a little under thirty minutes. The modern-day transatlantic air traveller can sit in his Boeing-made aluminium tube, fresh out of Heathrow, and cover the same journey in a fifth of that time. But both of them will fail to see the full beauty of the land over which they pass.

To behold and understand the true splendour of the Berkshire Downs, one needs to take the prehistoric M4 – the Ridgeway Path – described by some as the oldest road in the world. It runs, as the name suggests, along the edge of the limestone escarpment that crosses the southern British Isles from north-east to south-west. The Ridgeway itself stretches for eighty-seven miles, from Ivinghoe Beacon in the Chiltern Hills to Overton Hill near Marlborough in Wiltshire, crossing the river Thames at Goring. And it is the section to the south and west of this crossing with which I am most familiar, having lived in the village of Blewbury, near Didcot, for more than thirty years, until the middle of the 1980s.

The Berkshire Downs, or the North Wessex Downs as they are sometimes known, are part of the chalk uplands of southern England. Chalk is a sedimentary limestone rock created from the remains of millions upon millions of tiny marine creatures that once lived in a tropical sea during the Cretaceous period, some two hundred million years ago. The now rolling, grass-covered hills of Berkshire once lay deep beneath an ocean, at a time when the European continent of today sat astride the equator.

It is important to consider the geology of the area to understand why the Downs are so important for horse racing, the greatest love of my life. Just as in the state of Kentucky in the United States, the calcium-rich grasses that flourish on the limestone base produce good strong bones in the horses who eat it. The porous nature of the chalk also means that the rock acts as a reservoir of moisture during dry summers. This allows the grass to continue to grow green and lush, while that on the nearby London clay withers and browns.

In truth, the reason I adore the Downs so much is not as a result of any love I might have for geology. It was across their smooth undulating contours that I spent the best years of my life riding horses – toning their muscles and preparing them for the racecourse. How I loved the early spring mornings, with mist patches lying on the valley floor like fluffy white blankets. How I enjoyed the sun creeping up over the eastern horizon to bring warmth to the day. The vistas were spectacular, especially when viewed from horseback, through the gap between the ears of a galloping thoroughbred.

A CONVERSATION
WITH SELF

Trisha Goddard
on the woods

So when did you first fall in love with the woods?

I think it was when I was a little girl. I was in awe of them. But the woods have always had good PR, haven't they?

What do you mean?

Well, think of all those fairy tales that feature the woods: Babes in the Wood, the Big Bad Wolf stalking Red Riding Hood through the woods, Hansel and Gretel leaving a trail of breadcrumbs through the woods, Snow White hiding out with the dwarves in the woods . . .

OK – I get it! So what did the woods mean to you as a child?

The woods were somewhere I could go to escape. Kneeling on the bright green springy moss, pretending it was a fairy's lawn. Tiers of fleshy fungi clinging to the sides of knobby logs: a fairy block of flats. Holding my breath as my feet slowly crunched through dried twigs; listening . . .

Listening for what?'

Just listening . . . I know this sounds weird, but silence in the woods makes you feel small and watched. A scurrying of a squirrel. A burst of birdsong. Rustling. Those first spatters of fat raindrops on the leaves way above your head when you're safe and dry down here below . . .

So, almost fifty years later, here we are . . . still in the woods. But how come you're jogging through them, listening to music on your iPod?

Well, I do this every day. I need to. The music? It's my woods soundtrack! This song now? See the way the sun's streaming through the leaves? I can imagine me wearing some long medieval dress. I'm on horseback, ducking thick branches, galloping, yearning . . . And this song? I can dance to it; hopping over tree roots, kicking up little explosions of dried leaves, singing the chorus up to the bits of blue sky not obliterated by green. This next song? Well, it reminds me of the day they told me I had breast cancer. I came here, to the woods. I didn't cry then, but now in the safety of my woods, it's OK if I . . . you know.

I'm guessing that when the weather's bad, you give the woods a miss?

No way! The woods in snow – brilliant! Every so often you bump into a branch and get showered in snow. It's like confetti for the Ice Queen. See? In the woods I'm still that little girl! And in the rain I feel so smug; the leaves are sheltering me, but I can still hear those angry raindrops trying to get to me. Ha! On really windy days, my dog Alfie and I battle through the woods. Even though we're being whipped by stinging nettles and grit gets in our eyes, we have to struggle through because we alone can save . . .

Save whom?

It doesn't really matter. It's just that when all those massive trees start sighing, in my head I hear the voices of souls who will always be there. Trees are my inspiration. You know what they say about trees bending with the wind?

Yes?

In tough times I remind myself that 'Thy will be done'. If I don't learn to surrender to forces bigger than me, I'll snap like the brittle little twig I am out here.

You used a religious quote . . .

Ah, that's because the woods are my temple. I can push through the brambles, wired with worry about something or other. I guarantee that by the time I get to the stream, I'll be wondering what all the fuss was about! And then, when I get to the green on the other side, I have a solution. It's like subconscious praying . . .

You've stopped . . .

Yeah. I'm just looking. Breathing. Understanding. Back when I was a little girl? I think I left the spirit of the Child that Was in the woods. For safe keeping.

DEFENDERS OF OUR BACK YARDS

Zac Goldsmith
on Nimbys

If you really want to shame someone nowadays, you call them a Nimby. But I've never understood why. Nimbys are people who care about their local environment and who are willing to protect it. That's what the term means, and it's hard to imagine a more positive approach.

Of course, for the government and the big developers, Nimbys are an awkward obstacle to overcome. That's why the term itself was invented as a negative. When the House Builders Federation warns that 'Nimbyism is rampant', we know exactly where they're coming from.

Nor is it surprising that governments forever seek ways to defeat Nimbyism – invariably by moving the decision-making process as far away as possible from the people likely to be affected. For years locally-elected decision makers have been stripped of their powers and sidelined in local planning matters. Controversial local developments can be opposed by residents, opposed by elected councillors, yet still pushed through by unelected national quangos.

But what's harder to understand is why so many otherwise sensible people – campaigners, environmentalists, conservationists and so on – have allowed these self-evidently biased organizations to succeed in turning Nimbyism into a stigma. Why, whenever a local group criticizes a local development, does it feel the need to begin with the disclaimer, 'We're not Nimbys but . . .'?

Yes they are. And that's a good thing. Almost every river campaign, indeed most good environmental initiatives, happen because people want to protect the environment they know and love. Decisions affecting a local environment are always best taken by those living in that environment. So why should people be embarrassed about wanting to protect their own backyards?

There are unhelpful Nimbys, of course. Jealous campaigns to stop a neighbour improving his home, pointless crusades against a solar-roof installation. And there are times when Nimby campaigns have to be ignored in the interests of the wider country. But can you imagine what England would look like without them?

Those village greens, your local playing fields, the patch of ancient woodland, that stretch of river bank – all of them will have been eyed greedily by successive developers. These same treasures have been just as tempting to councils, which view them as untapped pots of money just waiting to be spent on yet more parking meters and no smoking signs. But if they're still there, there's just one reason – Nimbys.

If the Nimbys were in charge, we're told, the country would simply grind to a halt. But the collective wisdom of our Nimbys has proved far more advanced than that of our policy-makers. Take house-building. No one believes the planned house-building splurge on greenfield sites will solve homelessness, nor curtail house prices by more than a fraction of a per cent. So we'll see the permanent removal of our precious green spaces, and mounting pressure on water, because most of the current demand for housing is in the south-east, a continued 'brain drain' from the north. And all for a temporary non-solution.

No. If Nimbys were in charge, we'd see an effort to free the estimated 700,000 vacant homes on to the market before saturating our already crowded countryside with new builds. We'd see the introduction of US-style incentives to use the 75,000 acres or so of brownfield sites that are available for up to 1.5 million new homes.

The odds have always been against Nimbys. But they are the country's brakes on excess. We mustn't be embarrassed to call ourselves Nimbys. On the contrary, if we are not motivated to improve our local environment, that is far more shameful. After all – if we're not willing to stand up for our own backyards – who will?

AN ARTIST'S IMPRESSION

Andy Goldsworthy
on sheepfolds

AS AN ARTIST, I am often asked about the objects and locations that have directly influenced my work. For me, inspiration lies not in grand structures or celebrated monuments. It lies in a sheepfold at Winton in Cumbria's Eden Valley.

I first encountered this unimposing fold soon after moving to Brough in the early 1980s – most likely while on a walk up to the Nine Standards on Hartley Fell. It was early in my career and I had a part-time job working on the nearby Helbeck Estate, which involved doing minor repairs to dry-stone walls. I was still some years from using folds and walls as part of my art. But when I think of the Winton sheepfold and the impression it made on me, it is fair to say this farming structure has played a huge part in my creative life. It certainly kindled my interest in folds as sculptural forms.

The Winton fold is just a simple, circular form. But what I still find so striking is the way the fold is sited. It sits in an open space – a collection point for sheep grazing out on the fell – and it provides an extraordinary focus for its surroundings. As you walk off the fells from open ground into fields that gradually become smaller and more defined, the fold begins to feel like an earthbound oculus.

In the late 1990s, as part of the Sheepfolds Project, I rebuilt and repaired fifty existing sheepfold, washfold and pinfold sites in Cumbria. Unfortunately, even though I was keen to work on the site of the Winton fold – with several proposals made to the village – I was refused permission to do so. It seems this uncomplicated agricultural mark on the landscape will always remain just beyond my reach.

CHERRY TIME

Henrietta Green
on an endangered English fruit

WHY ARE CHERRIES SO appealing? Mention them and almost everyone breaks into a smile. Is it their cheery cherry-redness or glossy skin-shine, or the sheer joy of biting into such a small but perfectly formed fruit? Who hasn't decorated their ears with cherry earrings, stained their lips with cherry-juice lipstick or tinker-tailored the stones for a partner?

There is, however, little to smile about when it comes to the state of Britain's cherry industry. In the 1950s, when I was a child, cherry orchards covered 7,500 acres of the countryside. Travelling through Kent at the height of summer was cherry heaven with its roadside stalls laden with baskets, aka chips, filled with the freshly picked fruit. Now we grow less than a thousand acres, with home-grown cherries accounting for a mere 7.5 per cent of what we consume. In other words, 92.5 per cent of the cherries on sale, either fresh fruit or cherry-based products such as cherry pie or cherry brandy, are imported – even some of the fruit offered at the same roadside stalls.

What happened? The decline started in the late 1950s and was due, like almost everything in life, to a combination of factors. Let's start with the plague of birds and the state of our orchards. Most cherry trees in Britain were grown on old-fashioned root stock; as a result they were very tall, wide, stately and impossible to net. The fruit was unprotected and, not surprisingly, plundered – in some cases the trees were virtually stripped bare – by birds, mainly starlings. Starlings, for some inexplicable reason, were on the increase; if once you spotted a few, suddenly there were flocks of hundreds, even thousands. One fruit-grower even talked of how they 'shadowed the sun – so thick were they in the sky'.

Picking the cherries was also a problem; the rows of trees were too closely planted to allow machinery through, so they had to be picked by hand. Labour was difficult, no one seemed to want to pick any more, and it became more and more expensive. And then there were the imports. As trading regulations relaxed, cheaper cherries came from the sunnier, warmer European countries or from North America. One by one, the cherry orchards were left to decline or, worse still, grubbed up. Selling the land for housing was a far more attractive option than investing in modernizing an ailing industry – think how often you see a Cherry Lane or Cherry Corner housing estate.

Recently, however, cherry-growing has seen a revival, with new orchards being planted. Now it is all about new dwarf and frost-resistant rootstock that produces smaller, lower, more manageable trees, planted in wider regimented rows. These are grafted with new large commercial varieties – size really does matter here. Darker and fleshier than our traditional cherries, these lack the bright intensity of colour, the piercing fruitiness, the solid and firm texture and defined shape of my favourites. Try the pointy, heart-shaped, white-fleshed Elton Heart or the spicy, juicy Bigarreau Gaucher and you'll see what I mean.

Am I happy that growing cherries is on the increase? Well, yes and no. It reduces food miles, creates employment and I prefer to buy home-grown. But – and here's the rub

– in order to plant up these modern commercial orchards, some of the few remaining glorious, old-fashioned, chaotic orchards may have to go. And that would be a tragedy, not only for cherry lovers, but for the birds, bees, wild flowers and everyone who loves our English countryside.

PASTURES NEW

Graham Harvey
on species–rich grassland

ALONGSIDE OUR HOUSE ON Exmoor we have a small, steeply sloping pasture field known locally as 'the cliff'. The gradient is so lethal that no one has ever dared venture on to it with a tractor. And so it remains – unlike most grass fields in Britain – free from meddling hands, weedkillers and nitrate fertilizers. It's exactly the way nature intended.

In June, the field is festooned with wild flowers – rough hawkbit, clover, birdsfoot trefoil, known to the locals as bacon-and-egg, and burnet saxifrage. At times it looks more like a Constable painting than a serious place to produce food. Yet our small flock of Exmoor sheep thrives on it. And in summer the sward comes alive with grasshoppers, bees and flickering butterflies.

Now a forgotten feature of the English landscape, pastures like this were once commonplace. At every site, the precise mix of species was as distinctive as human DNA, with particular plants offering clues about the type of soil and climate. Chalk downlands might often have included rock rose, kidney vetch, scabious and wild thyme. And on the acid heathlands, fine-leaved grasslands could be found flecked with rue-leaved saxifrage and sheep's sorrel, with its tiny red flowers.

Whatever their precise composition, species-rich grass-lands were the handiwork of generations of craftspeople – the shepherds and graziers who managed them. They knew exactly when to allow the animals to graze, and when to take them off again. In so doing, they created living masterpieces.

Of course, such grasslands weren't intended as artworks. In fact, their beauty is a delightful by-product of the food production process. These were solar-powered engines of wealth creation, producing healthy foods in ways that were genuinely sustainable. They needed no fertilizers or pesticides to keep them productive. Nor were they dependent on diesel-guzzling machines. Yet, year after year, they turned out most of our beef and lamb; our poultry and eggs; our milk, butter and cheese.

Today we have turned our back on nature – choosing to produce these same foods by shutting animals in sheds and feeding them expensive grain. Without limitless supplies of cheap oil we would never have embarked on such a wasteful system. Now the price of oil is soaring – and with it, the cost of industrial grain. Soon we may have no choice but to give up our dependence on fossil-fuelled food and reclaim our neglected grasslands.

Returned to their former glory, these wonderful pastures will benefit both our nation's health and the health of the planet. Scientists have discovered that animals grazing traditional, species-rich grassland – including moorland pastures, heather moorland and saltmarshes – produce meat with higher levels of Vitamin E and heart-protecting omega-3 fatty acids than meat from modern grass monocultures. In addition, the meat from traditional grassland contains lower levels of saturated fat and higher levels of a powerful cancer-fighting compound known as CLA. And that's not all. Pasture farming also has a part to play in the struggle against climate change. While grain growing depletes soil fertility and releases carbon, grasslands safely store carbon as organic matter, even while they produce copious amounts of food.

Our predecessors knew a lot about making the countryside beautiful, sustainable and productive. And there's no reason why we – by recapturing our nation's pastures – can't do the same.

BONFIRE NIGHT

Tom Heap
on fires outdoors

To toss a dense mass of ivy into the blazing maw is to hear the gardener's equivalent of bursting bubble wrap. It crackles fiercely as though the fire itself was driven to grateful, riotous applause for such fuel. The moral satisfaction of destroying the creeping strangler adds to the pleasure, marred only a moment later when hot ivy-leaf cinders sting bare flesh.

But that is the sugar rush of bonfires. They also deliver more sustained nourishment to the outdoor soul. I grew up with a rambling garden of just over an acre that needed rigorous restraining. Such restraint began with the chainsaw and the axe but always ended, a few weeks or months later, with the bonfire. I watched my dad in the glow. I was taught respect for the magnetic danger of flames. He enjoyed the careful planning and feeding frenzy which makes a good flare-up. Grandpa, though, was the kind of allotment fire starter who could set flames in an unpromising sludge of old grass and garden debris, yet keep it smouldering for days, leaving only a perfect potash.

It is difficult to avoid nostalgia with bonfires. I guess it's the smell – the sense that delivers such solid linkage to the past it can feel like time travel. For me, the most powerful such sensation was at Glastonbury Abbey about ten years ago. It was a still November evening with a setting sun and a light mist evolving at eye level. The mist was infused with woodsmoke from an invisible bonfire. While I'm not given to New Age mysticism – in fact, I'm usually scathing – the scent delivered an immediate sense of history. I could almost smell the past. I fully expected King Arthur and Guinevere to emerge through a ruined arch.

Bonfire Night delivers a tangible link to the past, but it's the contemporary impact I treasure. If I ruled Britain, I'd make it a public holiday. Despite its historic divisiveness, I've found it to be one of our most inclusive festivals. When I lived in London, black and white, young and old, everyone took to the streets. It is the only national celebration when people leave their homes and take to the parks and fields to 'oooh' in harmony and 'aaah' in contentment. It's like a group hug for the emerging winter. Families in town and country thrill to an evening in the elements and enjoy a few hours outside.

Today I live in the country but lack sufficient space for a fire. Luckily, the local church needs their waste sent heavenward, so I still get my fix of woodsmoke, sparks and smoulder. I love it most powerfully at dusk – when the light vanishes but the fire still gives visibility. As the air chills, your back cools yet your face scorches. You wait to turn in the unburnt edges once more. You finally quit and walk home, leaving the fire behind. But the smoke stays with you, every thread of clothing carrying its aromatic signature: a reminder of the outdoors brought indoors. These days, when every conflagration is a source of climate concern, it could be considered a guilty pleasure; but pleasure it is.

FOLLOWING THE FURROW

Paul Heiney
on the ploughman

THE PLOUGHMAN IS A king amongst countrymen. At the end of every year he is the only man on the farm blessed with the power to take the fields, as if they were his own, and make them new again – how more sovereign can a man be than that? Tired earth, weary after an exhausting season supporting its crops, demands to be turned before it can begin its work again, and this is the ploughman's job. If the seasons are the leaves of the book of the farming year, it is the ploughman who turns the pages.

But when I think of rural royalty, perhaps I am thinking less of the modern tractor driver, insulated from the land by a foot of thick rubber tyre, isolated in his tractor cab, and more of the ploughmen who walked the fields behind horses, knowing every patch of land by the give of it beneath their boots. For a decade I ploughed with carthorses and there is no greater intimacy with the land than when following in the furrow, feeling through the handles of the plough the ever-changing ways of the soil.

Ploughing engages a man in many ways, although surprisingly strength is the least of it: horses do the heavy pulling and the ploughman has no need of pushing, for a finely tuned plough will glide through the soil with the ease of a wing through the air. The achievement of this sublime state, though, rests on experience. I counted thirteen different adjustments on a simple plough, each working together and making the setting of a plough as interactive as the tuning of a piano. But when all is correct, each nut perfectly tightened and every setting precisely made, then there is the possibility of a symphonic day behind the plough. All that can break the harmony are the horses.

Working horses are no slaves. They have minds of their own, and imaginations. If they get it into their heads that it is time for the midday break even though it is not yet ten o'clock, every furrow will be a fight as the ploughman asserts his will over theirs. Sometimes the fight can last all day. For devilment, a horse will deliberately lean against his mate and push him out of the furrow, causing the ploughman to curse. A sharp rebuke will bring him back to his senses, for a while, before his mischievousness finds another way to express itself.

Then there are the easy times when to plough with horses is to undertake a day-long conversation. A horse needs to hear you and know that you are there – his blinkers prevent him from seeing you. But how does this communication work? I have often called in a gruff voice, 'Get yo'self over, old hoss' and watched an old faithful take a step sideways, as asked, but I have no idea why he did it. But he certainly understood what I meant.

People have asked me if ploughing all day is lonely. How can it be? I talk more in a day's ploughing than in normal life, and to my remarks, projected the length of the reins, I seem to get answers, but I can't tell you what they are.

It is a mysterious business, to plough the land with horses. Those who have mastery of it are worthy of kingly respect.

CROSSING OVER

Leo Hickman
on cattle grids

'D-D-D-D-D-D-D-D-D.' As a boy growing up in Cornwall, I loved the sound of cattle grids.

Each time I saw one looming in the distance I would wince and grit my teeth in expectation of the fact that our family car would pass over it at several clicks faster than was probably recommended. Even now, it is the sound that comes to mind when I think about the countryside. I rank the percussive reverberations of rubber passing over metal bars at speed up there alongside the evocative call of the wood pigeon and the badger's bark.

And it seems I'm not alone. I smiled when I learnt recently that the sound had been judged important enough to be recorded and placed into the British Library's archives as an official soundscape – 'a sound that is pertinent to a place' – of Dartmoor. It delights me to know that, in decades to come, students will stumble across the digital recording of cars passing over the cattle grid between Princetown and Two Bridges.

What I really love about the sound, however, is what it symbolizes. It marks the border between a countryside that is tamed, neat and comforting, and one that is wild, tousled and close to danger. Cattle grids often tell us when we are entering common land – those fence-free stretches of common grazing that form some of England's most stunningly beautiful parcels of land. Cross a cattle grid and you can rest assured that, within a few minutes, a sublime moorland vista will present itself to you: a view of plaster-smooth undulations topped with granite, which have been maintained by countless generations of nibbling sheep, ponies, rabbits, deer and cows.

Cattle grids also represent ingenuity at its simplistic best. They perform that rare double act: an invention that offers perfect functionality – preventing animals straying while removing the bother of stopping a vehicle and opening a gate – without tainting, hindering or damaging its surroundings. Animals are instinctively wary of them, to such an extent that on some highways in the US, black and white stripes are painted on road surfaces to look like a grid to trick animals into not crossing them. Children are also unnerved enough by their sight to approach them with caution. (I always feared that I would get my leg stuck as I tentatively crossed them by foot, and that the local farmer would then need to fetch a saw to perform an amateur amputation in order to free me.)

For me, however daunting a prospect they appear, they will always be part of the landscape. But will evolution see their demise? It does seem some animals are trying cunning new ways to overcome these metal bars. In 2004, villagers in Marsden on the Yorkshire moors reported seeing hungry sheep lying on their backs and rolling across cattle grids so they could reach fresh pasture. 'Sheep are quite intelligent creatures and have more brainpower than people are willing to give them credit for,' responded the National Sheep Association to the news. If only we could all live in fear of cattle grids for ever – then this soundtrack to our countryside might never fade.

THE TREE MUSEUM

Simon Hoggart
on the National Arboretum

'They took all the trees
Put 'em in a tree museum
And they charged the people
A dollar and a half just to see 'em'

JONI MITCHELL SANG THAT in 'Big Yellow Taxi', a song about cherishing what you've got. And she'd be right about tree museums, except for the fact that, unlike a normal museum, an arboretum doesn't take its stock away from anywhere else. It creates its own, rather as if someone in a back room of the British Museum was turning out a constant supply of Saxon gold crowns and Roman amphorae. And as for cherishing what we've got, it would be hard to think of a better example than the National Arboretum at Westonbirt, just south-west of Cirencester. It is stunning, sensational, absolutely gorgeous: something which should delight every person in the country.

It is also vast, being six hundred acres and 1.7 miles from end to end. You can walk around it, but if you want to get the full flavour of the place you'll need to spend at least a day there, or rather several days during the different seasons. There are many other tree museums in the world – including the fine United States National Arboretum in Washington, DC – but I doubt if there are any as magnificent. Curiously, though some 350,000 people visit every year, it's nowhere near as famous and celebrated as many other national treasures.

One reason for the arboretum's captivating charm is that its founder, Robert Stayner Holford, was more interested in aesthetics than science. He inherited the estate, with Westonbirt House (a sort of oversized folly which is now a girls' boarding school), from his father in 1839. He also scooped a vast sum of money to go with the land. Holford was influenced by the fashion of the Picturesque movement and for bringing back rare and exotic plants from all round the world, mainly from the British Empire.

The result is that Westonbirt is not just a collection of trees, but a gigantic and cunningly designed park, with wide avenues, rides, narrow walkways, but also vistas, glades and groves. The trees are planted not merely where they will fit, but where they will be handsomely juxtaposed with their neighbours. Consequently, every corner you turn brings a new delight – perhaps something dark and small, with just a flash of colour, nestling close to the edge of a wide expanse leading down to the house, so that you can imagine a party of men on horseback cantering to dinner in a Jane Austen novel.

And what trees are here! There are sequoias, cedars, dogwoods, magnolias, rhododendrons, pine trees of every kind, from an incredibly rare Australian specimen to ones which tower higher than city of London office blocks. The busiest time of year is autumn (though the arboretum is so big that even if the car park is full, the place never seems crowded), when the acers, or maples, are in full scarlet, orange and yellow leaf. Westonbirt is one of the very few places in Britain that can compare with the glory of the American fall. With the low October sun penetrating the vegetation, the trees themselves seem to be on fire. One immense plane, its great black branches arching up and round and down until they touch the ground, creates a sort of flaming bell jar, or perhaps an Aladdin's cave in which the treasure lines every wall.

Lack of money and the exigencies of the Second World War meant that the family had to let go of the arboretum, and it has been run by the Forestry Commission ever since. Heed Joni's words and enjoy them, but it seems unlikely that anyone is going to pave this paradise to put up a parking lot.

HOW THE OTHER HALF LIVES

Charlotte Hollins
on cattle

I OFTEN THINK IT would be nice to live the simple life of a cow. I would spend the day munching various grasses and herbs from organic pastures and sitting down to chew the cud. Then, if I fancied a quick tipple, I would wander to the spring-fed pool, stroll into the woodland for a bit of shade from the hot summer sun before returning to graze the pastures again. It's all fairly tiring stuff!

My love of these domesticated ungulates stems from my earliest childhood memory. All I can remember is a vast landscape of grass, cows, and, of course, the inevitable cowpats. I grew up on an organic farm in rural Shropshire and was inspired by my late father, Arthur Hollins, whose passion for the English landscape knew no bounds. Arthur was an eccentric man with a true love for Mother Nature and everything she created. He was continually surprised and excited by the miraculous way in which nature just takes care of itself. And, every time I wander through our fields, so am I.

With its varied habitats, unpredictable wildlife and stunning topography, England spoils us. I love the fact there is always so much life to look at, wherever you are. I love the amazing way that each little bird, cow, small rabbit, each dungheap and tiny worm are all inextricably linked through the landscape; a landscape they have helped to create. I used to go for walks with my father and it wouldn't take long before he was down on his knees pulling apart a cowpat. He would talk for hours about the efficiency of worms in creating food for his pasture out of animal manure, and about the millions of other organisms that live in that hidden and somewhat magical world beneath the surface of every landscape we see. For him, that was what made the landscape real, and why diversity in his grass pastures and a sustainable extensive grazing system for his cattle became so important. I love this world of hidden dimensions he introduced me to – and the fertility it provides. Without it, I wouldn't be able to watch my wandering cows and escape from the characterless urban scene.

It is not hard to see the attraction of lazy days in the pastures. But you would be wrong to think of it as a mindless activity. For it is the intelligence of these gentle giants that really fascinates me. When a calf is asleep in the grass, visited by surrounding butterflies, the mother will go and graze in another area of the field. If she feels that danger may be approaching – such as an unsuspecting human – she does not walk up to her calf, but will often walk in the opposite direction to attract attention away from her baby. It's a great trick – unless you are a farmer trying to bring the cattle in for checking and need to find the calf.

Without a doubt, my favourite time of year is late spring, when the calves are born. As they are out all year, our cattle graze on nothing but grass and we are used to seeing them in the fields. But when the cows move into the summer water meadows and the calves arrive, there is nowhere in the world I'd rather be.

MY ISLAND

Elizabeth Jane Howard
on her river Waveney sanctuary

WHEN I WAS A child, I longed to be shipwrecked on an island. And I thought that to become the owner of one would be the height of exciting luxury. So when, about twelve years ago, I was able to buy the only island on the river Waveney – which borders my meadow – it felt like a dream come true. It was no tropical paradise – there was a small rickety bridge for access, about an acre of willows that had been regularly coppiced for fencing, some ancient apple trees, a wilderness of reeds and brambles and the largest ash I've ever seen. But it was my paradise.

Much had to be done to turn this patch of land into a vibrant habitat. The bridge had to be rebuilt. We made a fair-sized pond, which was stocked with fish, and a canal that ran from the pond to the drain at the far end. We cleared the way for a path and made three bridges over the canal. We introduced about thirty oaks (my favourite tree), mostly English but one or two red – the water table is so high they grew at exhilarating speed. We planted wild crab apple and plum trees of various kinds, three witch hazels, a number of lilacs, buddleia and roses – Kiftsgate, Veilchenblau, Paul's Himalayan musk and Bobbie James ramped up the old apple trees. There are half a dozen camellias, some viburnum, a tree peony, and the aconites, snowdrops, primroses, bluebells, *Fritillaria meleagris* and wild daffodils are steadily increasing.

We wanted to create something that could be enjoyed at all times of the year, with provision for as much wildlife as possible. There are now hedgehogs, grass snakes, rabbits, mice, camel-coloured frogs, reed warblers, thrushes, wood pigeons, sometimes a pair of owls, and a woodpecker. Some years we get butterflies attracted to the raucous mauve buddleia and a quantity of bees that love the ivy when it flowers. Ducks and a moorhen enjoy the pond and canal – the moorhen built her nest last year in the middle of a white waterlily that has assumed giant proportions. I also have a pair of mute swans called Bernard and Dora that have nested in various parts of the island and come in the summer to eat duckweed. Sadly, the first year Dora laid six eggs, they were stolen and the swans haven't come to nest again. I wanted the island to be a safe environment for nesting and I do hope they return.

The island is only small but it has become a magic place for me. I walk around it every day and there is always something to notice and love. People say we plant trees for others to enjoy in future. I think this is true, but the pleasure of watching them grow from saplings to fine young trees is a reward in itself. There is also a great satisfaction in introducing plants that, if they are happy, will naturalize. Cowslips seem exotic to me because I was brought up in Sussex where there weren't any, so to see them increasing every year is another plus. The arrival of the amazing and beautiful bee orchid was a thrill, but these flowers are mysterious and freakish in their behaviour; they will turn up one year and then disappear completely – and just as I have given up hope, appear somewhere quite different. They make plain the fact that wild flowers know what suits them, and cannot be tamed into putting up with conditions that garden plants often have to endure.

Of course, I have had failures. It is too wet for white foxgloves. Primulas do well, but the swans demolish them. Moles are a menace to the roots of young trees and mice eat the corms of anemones. But as my friend Ursula Vaughan Williams said, when she refilled a saucer of milk put out for a stray cat and found three slugs drinking from it, 'There's plenty for all.' And I hope my island will continue to be that for everyone who, in future, owns or lives on it.

AGAINST THE ELEMENTS

Margaret Howell
on protean shapes

Two photographs sit on my bookshelf. One shows the emaciated remains of Chanctonbury Ring after the 1987 storms wrecked its solid circle of beech trees. The other captures the skeletal wooden breakwaters of the east coast. Their imagery is similar – vertical, dark, abstract shapes in the landscape. Both are transformed from their original form into mysterious, beguiling objects.

An Iron Age fort dating from around the sixth century BC, ringed with a circle of beech trees planted in 1760, Chanctonbury Ring is a landmark that figured strongly in my childhood. Living on the edge of the North Downs as children, we would stand on a fine day and search the far horizon of the South Downs for its familiar outline. Many times we would climb the long chalk path and head for a picnic under the shade of its green leaves. Ancient, strong and dependable, it came to symbolize the Downs themselves, with their rolling lines and open skies.

But when, after the great storm, I saw the same trees stripped of branches, I recognized in their starkness the evocative power I now find in the solitary shapes scattered along our East Anglian beaches. Here too, on the edge, the landscape opens out. Reedbeds and saltmarshes merge with sea and sky; natural elements work on abandoned man-made forms, and the sea throws up the unexpected. Here one finds new forms, eccentric in their isolation, yet more powerful because of it. One can see an elemental beauty: one stick emerging from a strip of water; the geometric shape of a rusty gun emplacement; a single buoy out at sea and the stark uprights of those ravaged groynes sloping down into the waves.

Continually submerged then exposed, the groynes themselves – once rough-cut and squared to defend the beach – have lost their cross-beams, and the surviving posts have eroded into grained pinnacles that are sensual to the touch. Knots have loosened and fallen away, leaving smooth-edged holes as pure as a sculpture. These are man-made defences moulded by the very forces they set out to challenge.

There are other evocative forms, that speak of past times and purposes. The spiky, rusty remnants and broken concrete slabs of a pillbox left over from the Second World War can sometimes be seen – at other times it remains hidden under the constant shift of shingle. Here, even the beach itself is continually smoothed and raked into precise, sculpted ridges by the pull of the North Sea. Like the South Downs, this area can be seen as a purely abstract landscape. Long lines and flat, uninterrupted areas of land, sea and sky, where the slightest change in light is noticeable, convey the same awesome emptiness.

I can see why I keep these photographs together, but what makes them so iconic? Is it that they speak of our common past – of a people who would shape nature, are defeated by her, but then try again? Are they emblems of time and change and the need for acceptance? Perhaps it is because they prompt memories of one's own past? Or is it because of their sheer, fascinating beauty – not a romantic, quaint or picturesque beauty, but one that is clean, striking and, in every way, remarkable?

A REAL
CLIFFHANGER

Tristram Hunt
on the north Devon cliffs

Far removed from the deep England of the South Downs landscape or Chiltern Hundreds hamlets, stand the high cliffs of the north Devon coastline. Very different from the louche resorts and yachting inlets of the South Devon Riviera, this craggy coastline – which stretches from Woolacombe beach around to Minehead in Somerset – is an uncomfortable, nonconformist, dogged, bleak and utterly exhilarating part of England. Admittedly, there are few stately homes or well-tended gardens here, but there's certainly a sense of the island spirit.

Along much of this seascape meanders the excellent National Trust Neptune Pathway. But this is no Peak or Lake District thoroughfare with hundreds of people jostling from pub to B&B along well-worn paths. The steep, narrow routes and pummelling winds tend to reserve these walks for the hardiest souls. My favourite section runs from the elongated village of Combe Martin – once a noted mining, smuggling and strawberry-growing centre – to the elegant parades of Lynton and Lynmouth, Devon's so-called 'Little Switzerland', where Shelley, Wordsworth and Coleridge all found inspiration.

Along this edge of England, the cliffs rise up hundreds of feet tall, peaking with the arching sandstone of Great Hangman at just over 1,000 feet above sea level. Standing atop here, you can look one way across the Bristol Channel, another way to the bogs of Exmoor, and yet another to the western coastline. That is, if you can see anything at all. For most of the year, the mists and rain roll along this coastline in an unforgiving procession.

It is so damp that, in 1952, the inundated barrows began the terrible flow of water which led to the deadly Lynmouth flood. So this is a sodden scene of heath moorland, gorse and then, in the steep-sided valleys or combes which intercut the coastline, great beds of ferns and mosses among the small forests of oak.

But when the drizzle clears, what a sight it is! The crashing waves at Heddon's Mouth; the vertiginous cliff edges hurtling down to untouched beaches; the hillsides of bracken; and then the mysterious granite outcrop of Lundy Island shimmering in the distance. The animal life is also rich: between the sheep, the Exmoor ponies and the famous (or infamous) garden-eating Lynmouth goats, there are colonies of razorbill, guillemot and kittiwake, as well as black-billed gulls. And, if you are very lucky, you might see an adder sunning itself on the rocks, seals playing in the coastal swell and even the odd basking shark.

Above all, what the North Devon cliffs offer is a welcome sense of isolation and loneliness. Of course, man has made his mark here, stretching back to the Roman hill fort at Martinhoe on through the Victorian lime kilns to the mock-Tudor Edwardian lodging houses. But, today, bar the odd RAF flyby and spirited hiking party, the modern human footprint is enchantingly light. For the most part, it is you and the elements, you and the unforgiving sea – timeless geological formations, rushing streams, isolated coves and a sense of your own remarkable insignificance. It is, as I say, a rather different England.

CATHEDRALS OF SEWAGE

SEWAGE

Maxwell Hutchinson
on London's sewers

DOWN ABBEY LANE IN East London there sits a building that will never rank among the city's main attractions. Nobody notices its striking Byzantine-style elaborate flourishes or cruciform plan. Nobody misses its original two Moorish-style chimneys – they were demolished during the Second World War, condemned as a landmark for German bombers on raids over the city docks. But it is such a stunning building that its designers created two – its twin is situated at Crossness in south-east London. And because it's related to London's sewerage system, you'd hardly know it was there.

Even with this magnificent pumping station, otherwise known as a 'Cathedral of Sewage', the city's sewerage system is all but invisible – a secret underworld beneath London's bustling streets. But when you think that every sanitary appliance in the metropolis is connected to these secret brick tunnels, it is, in fact, far more intriguing and engaging than a life above ground. If you could only see this underground maze – as I have been privileged to do on several occasions – you would understand why it means so much to me. And why, in turn, it should mean so much to you. By removing waterborne disease, it is helping to keep us alive.

When the system was completed in 1875, London – along with most of the civilized world – had never seen anything like it. The city had grown exponentially following the Industrial Revolution, and the health, social and economic problems this brought meant that diseases such as cholera were threatening the population. The first outbreak occurred in 1831. It was generally believed that the disease was airborne, carried in a mysterious vapour known as miasma. Indeed, Florence Nightingale took this belief to her grave. The all-pervading fear of the miasma led the Victorians to drape their windows with heavy curtains in a vain attempt to keep the cholera at bay. The majority, however, drank the filthy water from the Thames, which was polluted with human sewage – most of the 369 sewers emptied into the river.

The problem was twofold: the quality of drinking water and the means by which sewage from the growing metropolis could be safely removed. In 1849, Dr John Snow, a physician from Soho who had carried out a survey of the health of those living within the catchment area of his practice, published the pamphlet, *The Mode of Communication of Cholera*. He had discovered that his patients who drank fresh well water from the pump in Broad Street, Soho, now Broadwick Street, didn't catch cholera. Those who drank from the local conduit, however, contracted the disease.

In parallel with Dr Snow's work, Sir Joseph Bazalgette convinced Parliament in 1858 to initiate the building of a gigantic network of underground sewers that would carry human effluent to the mouth of the Thames on the north and south banks. The effect of this massive endeavour on the health of Londoners was dramatic. Cholera epidemics were over for good.

The Bazalgette sewerage system was emulated through-out the civilized world. It was pioneering in every respect and remains as effective today as it was 130 years ago. So when I look at the wonderful Abbey Mills 'Cathedral of Sewage', I don't mourn the loss of its chimneys. I remember the people who made this innovative idea possible – and beautiful in the process.

THE WAY AHEAD

Kurt Jackson
on milestones

AT DUSK, ON THE way to the pub for an early evening pint, I hesitate and linger at a familiar spot in the valley near my home. For at the junction that connects No Go By Hill, Nancherrow Hill and the Kenidjack Valley, there is a milestone. If you look closely, this triangular piece of granite suggests that Morvah is four miles away, and Botallack just one. But unless you know where to look, you'd hardly know it was there.

Marginalized and squeezed out by a widened and surfaced lane, and now repeatedly slapped by the road run-off, car splash and gritting machines, this milestone has seen better days. The back of the stone is against a wall with hanging ivy, valerian and robin song (above, a robin is seducing me with her evening chorus) that supports a contemporary chevron. Bold, black and white, and unreservedly brash, it overshadows the older marker. The milestone seems almost invisible, especially now the kerbstone has been built up to meet it. Its granite faces seem to resist almost anything, with just the odd chip betraying its age. But, collecting litter and autumn leaves around its base, it looks as if it's lost its way.

There is something artistic about a milestone, but I am still unsure about its practical value. A coat of whitewash was once applied, and the pointing hands, letters and numbers that were carved into the surface have been filled with black pigment. It's all charmingly wonky, with almost childlike writing wrapped around the stone, as if the writer was running out of space. On other local examples where there wasn't enough room, the carver simply abbreviated the village names to become almost incomprehensible – other times they're misspelled or written out phonetically. How many strangers would have stumbled across them in their prime, and of what use would they have been with incorrect names? And why would locals who know directions and distances need a hand? I do think, however, it's a style particular to our parish. You only have to go a few miles away and the lettering and design changes – capitals replace that immature font, the hand vanishes and the stones are shaped differently.

This simple stone is almost forgotten and definitely ignored by most passers-by, a leftover from a time when travel was slow. Now the drivers are too fast and the pedestrians too familiar with it to pay any attention to its sharp edges or local detail. And even I must move on without its guidance. The robin has stopped singing, I'm getting cold, and I'm going to catch that pint. For the pub I'll take the unsigned way opposite, up Nancherrow Hill.

TO THE MANOR BORN

Simon Jenkins
on English country houses

HONSDON HOUSE

A FEW YEARS AGO, I travelled around England with one purpose: to write about its country houses. England has a greater number of houses with their contents intact and on public display than any other country in the world. Designed by a roll call of eminent architects – Inigo Jones, Nicholas Hawksmoor, Christopher Wren – they reflect the aesthetic styles of their time, from the peles, keeps and heraldic halls of medieval England, to the eaves and cupolas of the Jacobean tradition, and the splendour of the Classical revival.

I walked Vanbrugh's Long Library at Blenheim Palace, the marble pavements of Castle Howard and the exquisite cube rooms of Wilton. I looked out over Beaulieu's river through windows cusped with tracery, examined the murals and scrollwork of Knole's great staircase and explored the green damask dressing rooms of Holkham Hall.

My research also led me to houses that are less grand. East to Charles Dickens's so-called Bleak House in Kent, where the sea winds blow and gulls occasionally fall down the chimneys by mistake; south to Thomas Hardy's villa in Dorchester, where his second wife typed out his love poems to her predecessor; and north to the slopes of Skiddaw, where in the bee garden of Mirehouse Manor, Tennyson found refuge after the death of a friend.

I paid no less attention to the grounds of country houses; peaceful places with their graceful lawns, pollarded lime walks and meadows of wild flowers. The gardens of Levens Hall in Cumbria are sculpted with yew and box topiary, while those at Mapperton House in Dorset billow down the hillside, intersected by arbours and Ham stone walls.

All English houses, grand or otherwise, are in essence homes – refuges from the world, where people loved, lived and died. They are places of solace as well as of function; a conversation between utility and beauty. The Englishman sees the whole of life embodied in his house. Here he finds his happiness and his real spiritual comfort, as observed by the German architect Hermann Muthesius.

Today, while many English country houses allow us an insight into the artistry of previous eras, their utility also prevails. Tregothnan Estate in Cornwall is an official safe site for the protection of endangered trees from all over the world, while Waddesdon Manor in Buckinghamshire contains one of England's finest composite collections of art and antiques, and Chatsworth has one of the largest private libraries. At Christ's College, Cambridge, I found the perfect embodiment of utility and beauty: a mulberry tree, planted at the time of James I to help the English silk trade, still in flower.

Old houses offer us communion with the roots of England, a collective narrative of its history. But they must continue to breathe, and not be preserved as museums or mausoleums. William Morris, who cherished Kelmscott Manor in Oxfordshire with a passion, believed that we are only the trustees for those who come after us. As such, we must ensure that we never allow the spirit of English country houses to suffocate under dust sheets or die in the gloom of a shuttered room. They are exquisite tributes to their time, our portals to the past.

VIEW OVER
LONDON

Terry Jones
on Hampstead Heath

IT ISN'T REALLY A heath, only half of it lies in Hampstead and East Heath is actually on the West, but so what? Hampstead Heath is still, to my mind, the ultimate evocation of perfect English countryside.

It helps that it almost exactly matches the imaginary countryside of my childhood, as depicted by Alfred Bestall in the Rupert books, with its gentle, grass-clad hills dotted with occasional trees and tangles of woodland. The idyllic rustic playground – just as nature intended. But, of course, Hampstead Heath – like Rupert's Nutwood – is an invention.

In medieval times the Heath was a true heath, made up of easily dried-out, sandy soil supporting scrubby vegetation. Its summit was the sandy ridge linking Hampstead and Highgate villages. It still retained the character of moorland when John Constable painted it between 1819 and 1837. Constable depicts fewer trees than there are now, interspersed with patches of heather and gorse, and the distant views of London are uninterrupted by hedge or thicket. But Constable also paints another aspect of Hampstead Heath that is perhaps more surprising.

He shows it as a place of industry, with men hard at work excavating the fine sand which, at one time, covered the entire surface of the Heath up to a depth of ten inches. The level of excavations on the Heath was such that, in 1806, there were complaints that the resulting pits were dangerous and 'the whole face of the heath is become so mutilated that the prospect of beauty is nearly destroyed'.

This disfigurement of the Heath reached its zenith

in the 1860s. The much-reviled Sir Thomas Maryon Wilson had spent thirty fruitless years attempting to assert what he considered his right to build on his own land and to lease building land on the Heath, which he controlled as Lord of the Manor of Hampstead. Finally, when the Midland Railway extended its line to St Pancras and needed huge quantities of gravel and sand, he seized his chance to turn the land to profit. To supply the railway company, Sir Thomas devastated the Heath on both sides of Spaniards Road, digging pits as deep as twenty-five feet. He destroyed the heather, gorse, broom and trees to such an extent that the area to the west of Spaniards Road has never recovered.

What's more, in his desperation to turn his estate to profit, he leased a large section of it (from the viaduct down to the valley of the Hampstead Ponds) as a brickfield. Sir Thomas's character was such that I imagine he derived a grim pleasure from the thought that, since he wasn't allowed to build on the Heath, he wouldn't allow it to be the place of beauty that his opponents claimed it to be.

But then the truth is that the Heath had always been valued more for its natural resources than for its beauty. Gravel and loam were extracted for many years, and it was also used for turf-cutting and the grazing of animals. There were sheep grazing on the Heath as late as 1952.

The Heath was also famous for its many springs, and Hampstead and Highgate brooks were two of the main tributaries of the Fleet river, but there were no actual ponds on Hampstead Heath until 1692, when the Hampstead

Water Company created the first two as reservoirs to supply water to London.

So even the famous Hampstead and Highgate Ponds are not natural, and the appearance of the Heath today is as much a man-made artefact as Blenheim Palace or Kew Gardens.

But then the Heath doesn't *have* to be a work of nature. To tell the truth, I think it's an improvement on nature: an ideal countryside that you only find in dreams or in children's stories.

OLDER THAN ENGLAND

Paul Kingsnorth
on the Green Man

I HAVE SEEN HIS face everywhere, for longer than I can remember. High up on the stone roofs of great cathedrals. On the bench-ends of ancient pews. Carved into the lintels of churches from the last millennium. In the pages of books and on websites and sometimes, it seems, in the trees themselves at night in high summer. He is older than the trees; older, probably, than England itself. But he is still out there.

He is the Green Man, and his face can be seen carved into churches all over England, in a thousand variants. At his most basic he is a human face surrounded by woodland foliage. In his more pagan, florid guise, his mouth, eyes and nose sprout leaves, shoots and branches. Sometimes he is sinister. Sometimes he is comical or beguiling.

Who is he? We don't know. What we do know is that this symbolic melding of Man and Nature is very ancient indeed. Some have speculated that he is the remnant of some ancient fertility cult; others that he is a devil or a god. Some believe he is a Christian symbol; others claim him for the Druids, the Anglo-Saxons, the builders of prehistoric monuments.

Why is he here? Again, we don't know. Green Men are not a specifically English phenomenon: they can be found, in various guises, all over Europe and as far afield as Nepal, Mesopotamia and Borneo. But why is he most commonly found in England, in old churches? Is he a representation of the Devil – the Church playing its old trick of coopting pagan gods to represent its own version of evil? Is he a snook being cocked at Christianity by pagan-minded stone workers? Is he even – my favourite theory – a symbol of political resistance? Green Men occur most notably in Norman churches, and it has been suggested that they were representations in stone of English resistance to the Norman Conquest of 1066. For a decade after that date, English rebels were at large in the forests, fighting a guerrilla war against their new masters. The Normans called them *silvatici* – men of the woods. Did stonemasons who supported the rebels carve their faces into the new Norman buildings in solidarity?

Perhaps. But in the end the Green Man is an archetype, as old as the downs and the dales. He is all of us, and he reminds us of our place in the landscape and its place within us. In an age of environmental crisis he still watches over us; chides us, perhaps, for what we have become and what we are doing. He takes us back to basics: back to the green wood where all life is born and to where it will all, eventually, return.

DOWN MEMORY LANE

Miles Kington
on the family historian

SOMETIMES YOU CAN STILL see him, as dusk approaches, trudging along a country lane with the tools of his ancient trade dangling round him. He'll have his bags of notebooks, his laptop computer in its neat waterproof case, and condensed county guides and parish registers, sometimes reduced to the abstracted wisdom of a CD-ROM.

He is, of course, the family historian, driven by his quest for arcane knowledge and by the compulsion to explore his own family history. He is not always a welcome figure. Sometimes remote householders will peer out through their curtained windows and hastily draw the drapes shut as they see him come along the lane, pulling one of those trolleys used by fishermen, to transport all that genealogical knowledge. More often, clergymen with lone churches in their care, full of irreplaceable books of deaths, births and marriages, will spot him coming and shiver. They know that once the family historian is ensconced in a church, he may be there for days or weeks. Or even months.

Usually, there is just one family historian to each family. Nobody knows why, but each family seems to produce just the one member who acquires the urge to chart the furthest nooks and crannies of his own family tree. The rest of the family, if they ever had the incentive to follow the thin lines of descendants and forebears, are now quite happy to leave it to him.

It is nearly always a 'him'. Very rarely does the family historian turn out to be a woman. Women are interested in people as people, not as strange names on a document. The gene that turns men into trainspotters, or into car experts, or into founts of knowledge about the personnel of jazz groups, must also be the one responsible for transforming them into family historians.

And so he comes to build up the map of the family. The family historian is very good at asking the little questions (such as 'When Uncle Jack went off to make his fortune in Australia, is there any clue that he ever came back again?' and 'Who is this little bloke who keeps cropping up in family photos between 1920 and 1935 – his name is always crossed out so heavily that we don't know who he is?'), but not so good at asking the big questions (such as 'What on earth am I asking all these stupid little questions for?').

I feel that being a family historian is an ancient craft, and that most of the old and grand families of England would have had their own archivist to keep the family tree in order. He might well have turned up as a character in a P. G. Wodehouse novel.

> *'I say,'* said Cousin Augustus, *'who's that queer cove wandering around in the library, wearing a moustache that wouldn't look out of place in the shellfish section of a fishmongers?'*
>
> *'Oh,'* said Aunt Mildred, *'that's young Wesley Snape. Your uncle has hired him to come and sort the family out.'*
>
> *'Sort the family out? What's wrong with the family?'*

'There's a whole lot of cousins missing in New Zealand in about 1890,' said Aunt Mildred.

'Good God,' said Cousin Augustus. 'Mass murder, was it?'

'No,' said Aunt Mildred. 'Missing page in the family chronicle. Your uncle wants them all brought back and identified . . .'

But, of course, family historians do not turn up in modern novels. A novelist makes things up, and that would be anathema to a family historian. The noblest thing a family historian can do is go on lugging his family documents around with him, through the back lanes of old England, dragging back from obscurity characters that nobody ever knew existed in the first place.

EARTH PILGRIM

Satish Kumar
on Dartmoor

MY LIFE IS AN unending pilgrimage – I have no destination. Touching the earth – being connected to the soil, being mindful of every step – is how I practise eco-spirituality. Walking in the wild is my meditation. Walking in nature is my prayer, my peace and my solitude. Breathing, I inhale the air, which sustains me and connects me to all life.

Dartmoor is my temple and my church – a glorious cathedral of nature – that is millions of years old. It was formed by the powers of geological time and the generosity of nature. I come here for the breath of fresh air, the smell of the wet grass, the coolness of water and the purity of rocks.

I often make my pilgrimage to Wistman's Wood, high up on the eastern moor. It's an ancient oak grove that Druids made their place of worship thousands of years ago – the name Wistman's Wood means 'Wise man's Wood'. The trees here hold firm to the earth to show us the resilience of life at high altitude, six hundred metres above sea level on the windy moors. They grow through massive slabs of granite. Local myths and legends speak of 'nature spirits' inhabiting these woods. When everything looks dry and dormant, lichen and moss thrive. Life is vibrant here. One species of lichen that lives in this wood can be found nowhere else on earth. It is exquisite, a vital link in the interconnectedness of all living things.

These woods are sparse now. Once, much of the moor was covered in oak. Now there are only remnants of the ancient forest – the wood's aura of light and shade. It is a place of mystery, memory and meaning, and I feel at one with this primeval paradise. I find these trees loving, compassionate, still, unambitious and enlightened. In eternal meditation they give pleasure to a pilgrim, shade to a deer, berries to a bird, beauty to their surroundings, health to their neighbours, branches for fire and leaves to the soil. They ask nothing in return, in total harmony with the wind and the rain. The trees are my mantra, my poem and my prayer. Through them, I learn about unconditional love and generosity.

Mistletoe – a sacred plant – grows high on the trees when everything else is dormant. It is a celestial gift, the marvel of life in the darkness of winter. There is a symbiosis between the thrush and this plant. The mistle thrush's song signals love as a biological imperative. Give the gift of kisses under mistletoe and your love will be eternal.

The Buddha would sit under a tree for hours in his renowned posture, touching the earth with the fingertips of his right hand. This symbolizes reverence for the earth and recognition that everything – our body, our knowledge and wisdom – comes from and returns to the earth. Someone once asked the Buddha from whom he learnt the virtue of forgiveness. The Buddha pointed towards the earth. That became his famous posture and gesture.

The oak wood below, lightning above and thunder all around, are part of the great mystery of nature. All the science, philosophy and poetry of the world put together cannot explain the ultimate meaning of existence. And I am happy to live with this mystery.

WRITING STILES

David Lodge
on stiles

THERE IS NO OBJECT more emblematic of rural England than the stile. Although I suppose other countries have them, they are especially characteristic of the English countryside, with its patchwork of fields bounded and protected by hedgerows and fences. But, of course, a stile is more than a utilitarian device for passing from one field to another. There are no urban stiles and to me, a child who first encountered country life during the Second World War as a displaced Londoner, stiles were novel and amusing structures, such as one might find in a playground. For adults, too, they have many uses: one may sit on them, stand on them, lean on them, use them for flirtation and courtship, conversation or confrontation. Symbolically, they are liminal objects, marking a threshold – the passage from one state to another. The classic English novelists were well aware of these possibilities. In *Jane Eyre*, for instance, the heroine first encounters Mr Rochester while sitting on a stile, where she has paused in the middle of a winter walk:

> *I sat down on a stile which led thence into a field. Gathering my mantle about me, and sheltering my hands in my muff, I did not feel the cold, though it froze keenly; as was attested by a sheet of ice covering the causeway . . .*

Along comes Mr Rochester on his horse, which slips on the ice, throwing its rider to the ground. Jane helps him up and, leaning on her, he hobbles over to the stile and sits down.

In the conversation that follows, he identifies her as the governess who has come to look after his ward. She helps him remount, and goes on to complete her errand, musing on the incident:

It was an incident of no moment, no romance, no interest in a sense; yet it marked with change one single hour of a monotonous life.

In fact, it has momentous consequences. It is Jane's unflustered helpfulness in their first encounter which leads Rochester to fall in love with her, by imprinting her on his consciousness as his rescuer in need, just as she will be at the end of the story.

In the Victorian age, when women were swathed in clothing from head to foot, the act of negotiating a stile – and thus showing an ankle or a flash of petticoat to accompanying males – was full of possibilities for coquetry and gallantry. There is a delightful example in *The Pickwick Papers*. Mr Pickwick and his companions, walking across the fields to Dingley Dell for the Christmas celebrations, meet Mr Wardle and his daughter, Emily, accompanied by a bevy of young ladies. Introductions take place without formality:

In two minutes thereafter, Mr Pickwick was joking with the young ladies who wouldn't come over the stile while he looked – or who, having pretty feet and unexceptionable ankles, preferred standing on the top rail for five minutes or so, declaring that they were too frightened to move. It is worthy of remark, too, that Mr Snodgrass offered Emily far more assistance than the absolute terrors of the stile (though it was full three feet high and had only a couple of stepping stones) would seem to require; while one black-eyed young lady in a very nice little pair of boots with fur round the top, was observed to scream very loudly, when Mr Winkle offered to help her over.

The most striking use of a stile, however, must be in Hardy's *Tess of the D'Urbervilles*. When Tess, who has been seduced by Alec D'Urberville and is with child, is walking sadly back to her home village, she is overtaken by an artisan, carrying a pot of red paint. It is a Sunday morning. 'All the week I work for the glory of man,' he says, 'and on Sunday for the glory of God . . . I have a little to do here at this stile.' He stops, dips his brush in the paint pot, and . . .

> *. . . began painting large square letters on the middle board of the three composing the stile, placing a comma after each word, as if to give pause while that word was driven well home to the reader's heart – 'Thy, Damnation, Slumbereth, Not.'*
>
> *Against the peaceful landscape . . . these staring vermilion words shone forth . . . Some people might have cried 'Alas poor theology' at the hideous*

defacement . . . But the words entered Tess with accusatory horror. It was as if this man had known her recent history; yet he was a total stranger.

The English countryside had a better class of vandal in those days.

BLUEBELL PICNICS

Gabby Logan
on Kew Gardens

I AM A CITY girl born in Leeds, raised in Leeds for a while and then on to Coventry, with a year in Vancouver in the middle. The wonderful thing about being a child in most cities in the UK is that glorious countryside is never far away, not some intangible thing you can only read about in books. So although my farmer husband teased me about being a 'townie' when we met, I was quick to point out that I had been privileged enough to live on the doorstep of some of this country's most beautiful landscapes: the Yorkshire Dales and the Cotswolds for two. In short, I may not have been adept at milking a cow but I knew good countryside when I saw it.

We now live in London, well, technically it's Surrey, but we are five minutes' walk from the Tube and two minutes' walk from the Lion Gate entrance to Kew Gardens. To me that sentence sums up what it is to have the best of both worlds. I realize how lucky I am, and it's my love of Kew I would like to share with you. I did wrestle with Richmond Park for a while, but discounted it because it's more than three minutes from my front door.

I write this in September, a particularly exciting time of the year in Kew Gardens. The trees are starting to turn and in about three weeks there will be a day when the sun is in the corner of the sky looking like it doesn't really want to bother coming out for a while, and it will cast a red light on the canopy of trees, so even the grass will look like an orange shade of green. The coaches and buses parked outside the Gardens with their Cardiff, Carlisle and Cornwall phone numbers on the side are testament to the joyous sight that Kew is in September; people will drive for hours to take in the experience.

There is one afternoon in particular I remember, when the children and I went collecting fallen conkers, and then we acted out scenes from *The Wizard of Oz*. It was the most natural thing in the world to do. Now, Kew Gardens is quite strict, no bikes, no scooters and no balls, but as long as you respect the plants and the trees, you can pretend to be the Tin Man or Dorothy all day long. Sit and think, walk and talk, learn and discover or play; just don't try getting a scooter past those men in bottle-green uniforms at the entrance.

In the summer we took the Scottish cousins, who still live on a farm, for a picnic in a secluded corner of the Gardens. We didn't see another face for an hour, and this was the height of the school holidays. The spot we had chosen was like something from a Lewis Carroll novel; we played hide and seek for hours in meadow grass with wild flowers around us.

Sometime in spring we'll wander through the Gardens, we might be on our way home from school, and the carpet of purple crocuses will be out and we'll all stand and stare in amazement at their beauty, while equally impressed tourists take pictures and video the scene because they may never get back to Kew.

Sure, Kew Gardens is known for its Lilac Garden and its Azalea Garden and its Japanese Gardens, and of course the Orangery and the Temperate House are very impressive. While I love all of these, I think I am happiest in the slightly more rugged conservation area, where the bluebells pop up in random fashion and the crowds tend not to go.

HIDDEN DEPTHS

Richard Mabey
on marshland

AT A CASUAL GLANCE, it seems the very negation of landscape. Nothing blocks the view to the horizon. There are no elevations, no shadows and no secret glades. The ground seems to have been scoured into a rumpled, homogeneous plain.

But marshland is more subtle than that. Think of it, for a moment, as a landscape whose contours are under the ground – as an inverted habitat, riddled with concavities. Then imagine it turned upside down. Now the prospect is alive with mounds and reticulations. Glacial hollows and human peat pits swell like prehistoric barrows. Dykes are three-dimensional fences. Peat layers appear and disappear in complex laminations.

Now turn it upright again. Think of the whole surface of the marsh as an outgrowth of this damp labyrinth. Resist the pull of the horizon and shorten your focus a little. The homogeneity vanishes. There are dark sedges, livid bog mosses and lustrous mist-green patches of reed. There are grass tussocks, scrubby tumps, pools and inscrutable ribbons of vegetation. And, closing your focus still further, you realize that this apparently bland and static view is in constant motion. Marshes – mosaics of thin verticals – are animated by the wind like no other landscape.

Now think of the birds that coast above marshlands as dowsers of this complex geometry of wetland and wind. Ducks explode into the air, manifesting patches of water that, to the watcher, are quite invisible. Marsh harriers tack across the fens, rising and falling as if they were riding invisible currents in the air – pockets of low pressure, tiny thermals generated by the minute shifts from water to grass to reed. Once, in Suffolk, I watched a hobby riding the subtle troughs in a reedbed like a surfer. It was catching dragonflies, and as it soared up to eat them, the chitin from the chewed-off wings fell back into the reed like tinsel. The whole vocabulary of the marsh is about this intimacy of movement: rustling, gliding, quaking, shimmering.

Nothing, however, animates marshland more than the water that created it. When the rains come (the winter floodtime), water finds its way back into the shallowest dips and into every inch-deep depression, remaking the landscape it formed ten millennia ago. And the shapes it makes seem amorphous and unbiddable. It slinks about the surface of land like a Chinese whisper, full of possibilities, taking new form as it goes – joining field puddle with reed pool, with streamlet, with river.

Marshlands are the stage for fast-moving dramas of the great principles that govern ecosystems: change, continuity and connectivity. Water is an excellent communicator and forms a conduit for reed seeds and migrating eels, between ancient habits and new beginnings. Sometimes, when I walk on a marsh, efflorescences of water spread round my feet, and yards, maybe miles, further on I have the feeling that I'm squeezing water out on to some slumbering aquatic growths. Marshes may momentarily look inert and vacuous, but in reality they are agile, adaptive and inclusive. They are about living in the present and going with the flow.

A GUARDIAN OF BEAUTY

Fiona MacCarthy
on William Morris's Kelmscott

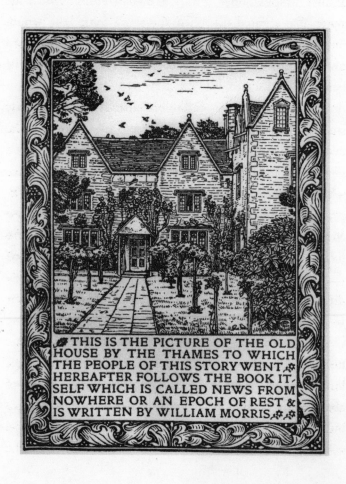

THIS IS THE PICTURE OF THE OLD HOUSE BY THE THAMES TO WHICH THE PEOPLE OF THIS STORY WENT HEREAFTER FOLLOWS THE BOOK IT SELF WHICH IS CALLED NEWS FROM NOWHERE OR AN EPOCH OF REST & IS WRITTEN BY WILLIAM MORRIS

KELMSCOTT MANOR IS A gabled grey stone house in the flat meadowlands between Faringdon and Lechlade. It stands at the furthest end of a small village, where a farm track transforms itself into the towpath of the river Thames. William Morris, the poet and designer who lived there from 1871 to his death in 1896, described Kelmscott as 'a beautiful and strangely naïf house'. To him it had an almost mystic quality of Englishness, the unselfconscious sense of craftsmanship and total visual rightness, which inspired some of Morris's most marvellous design work and sustained him through a turbulent, courageous personal life.

Even now, though Kelmscott village has been greatly smartened up, you can see what Morris saw in it when he first arrived there looking for a country retreat from the stresses of his London decorating business, and a place where his friend, the painter Dante Gabriel Rossetti, could be discreetly alone with Morris's wife Janey. William Morris was the model of the unpossessive husband. The unassuming manor in the out-of-the-way village was the answer to his dreams, and, curiously, he had actually dreamed of a building just like Kelmscott before he ever viewed it in reality.

Architecturally, Kelmscott was Morris's ideal. The house was built mainly in the mid-sixteenth century for a local farming family, using the coarse local oolite stone of the Thames Valley. This was practical necessity for country builders, what Morris called 'the liking for making material serve one's turn'. The stone was well laid and then, as he put it, 'buttered over' with thin plaster which gradually weathered to the same colour as the walls. The designer in him particularly appreciated the way in which the stone slates for the roof had been carefully sized down by the roofers, using small ones at the top and large towards the eaves, creating a design of natural beauty like the pattern of bird feathers or fish scales.

Morris looked for an organic quality in buildings, a sense of rootedness and permanence. He loved Kelmscott's ancient history, the way it seemed almost to have 'grown up out of the soil and of the lives of those who lived there'. He gloried in its intimate connection with rural economics and the natural activities of the English countryside: the bleating sheep surrounding Kelmscott Manor became his favourite creatures in the world. Morris drew on the English country flowers in his garden and the wild plants of fields and hedgerows: the plenitude of natural forms he found around him for the textiles he produced in a surge of creativity in the 1870s. The willows overhanging the stretch of the Thames running through his land at Kelmscott gave him the motif for his still most popular wallpaper design.

Kelmscott came to acquire a sacred meaning for Morris. The treacherous Rossetti was eventually ejected as having 'ways unsympathetic' to those of the old house. When Morris moved into his London home in Hammersmith this too was (confusingly) known as Kelmscott House, and he liked to imagine making journeys from Kelmscott to Kelmscott up the Thames. He also adopted Kelmscott as the name of his private printing press, the Kelmscott Press.

When, towards the end of his life, William Morris wrote his great visionary novel, *News from Nowhere*, the journey towards utopian perfection ends at a place that is obviously Kelmscott: 'The blackbirds were singing their loudest, the doves were cooing on the roof-ridge, the rooks in the high elm-trees beyond were garrulous among the young leaves, and the swifts wheeled whizzing about the gables. And the house itself was a fit guardian for all the beauty of this heart of summer.'

An iconic English scene indeed.

THE ROAD TAKEN

Robert Macfarlane
on holloways

THE WORD 'HOLLOWAY' COMES from the Anglo–Saxon 'hola weg', meaning a harrowed path, a sunken road. It is a route that centuries of use has eroded down into the bedrock – so much so that it is recessed beneath the level of the surrounding landscape. Most will have started out as drove roads, paths to market; some, like those near Bury St Edmunds, as pilgrim paths.

These sunken roads are landmarks that speak of habit rather than suddenness. Trodden by innumerable feet, cut by innumerable wheels, they are the records of journeys to market, to worship, to sea. Like creases in the hand or the wear on the stone sill of a doorstep or stair, they are the consequence of tradition, of repeated action. Like old trees – the details of whose spiralling and kinked branches indicate the wind history of a region, and whose growth rings record each year's richness or poverty of sun – they archive the past customs of a place. Their age humbles without crushing.

The oldest holloways date back to the early Iron Age. None is younger than three hundred years old. Over the course of centuries, the passage of cartwheels, hooves and feet wore away at the floor of these roads, grooving ruts into the exposed stone. As the roads deepened, they became natural waterways. Rain drains into and down them; storms turn them into temporary rivers, sluicing away the loose rock debris and cutting the road still further below the meadows and the fields.

Holloways do not exist on the unyielding igneous regions of Britain, where the roads and paths stay high, riding the hard surface of the ground. But in the soft-stone counties of southern England – in the chalk of Kent, Wiltshire and East Anglia; in the yellow sandstone of Dorset and Somerset; in the greensand of Surrey and in the malmstone of Hampshire and Sussex – many are to be found, some of them twenty-feet deep; more ravine than road. In different regions they go by different names – bostels, grundles, shutes – but are all holloways.

Of course, few are in use now. They are too narrow and too slow to suit modern travel. But they are also too deep to be filled in and farmed over. So it is that, set about by some of the most intensively farmed countryside in the world, the holloways have come to constitute a sunken labyrinth of wildness in the heart of arable England. Most have thrown up their own defences, becoming so densely grown over by nettles and briars that they are unwalkable, and have gone unexplored for decades. On their steep damp sides, ferns and trailing plants flourish: bright bursts of cranesbill, or hart's tongue, spilling out of and over the exposed network of tree roots that supports the walls.

I think of these holloways as being familial with cliffs and slopes and edges throughout Britain and Ireland – with the Cliffs of Moher in County Clare, or the inland prow of Sron Ulladale on the Isle of Harris, or the sides of Cheddar Gorge or Bristol Gorge, where peregrines nest. Conventional plan-view maps are poor at registering and representing land that exists on the vertical plane. Cliffs, riverbanks, holloways: these aspects of the land go unnoticed in most cartographies, for the axis upon which they exist is all but invisible to the conventional mapping eye. Unrecorded by maps, untenanted by humans, undeveloped because of their steepness, these vertical worlds add thousands of square miles to the area of our country – and many of them are its wildest miles.

DRAWING THE LINE

Andrew Marr
on lines

THERE ARE WILD PLACES. But they are not the essential England. This is an old, moist, busy, rubbed-over, scored, loved-and-plundered place whose character comes from human intervention, not in spite of it. An icon of Englishness, this Scot thinks, is the line.

There are so many lines. There's the hard-won, strong-built property line of the dykes of Yorkshire, Northumberland and Derbyshire. Everywhere there are lines of old fields from the air, rising like undersea markings when the crops grow. Deep-driven lines of Devon bridlepaths are so gouged in the pink clay they become semi-submerged tubes of greenness in the summertime. There are the lines of copses, cut neatly round just where the tilt of the field means the combine harvester can't clutch – leaving upended pudding bowls of beech or ash across the south. There are the harvest lines themselves, parallel machine trails of dark brown on silvery gold; the energetic thrust lines of old industrial canals, and the lines of Victorian and Edwardian railways – bold, hacked lines made by Irish labourers, many of which are now as grassed and quiet as Neolithic barrows. There are the vertical stub lines of dead industrial chimneys and the parallel lines of coal and cotton towns, hanging on to their hillsides, as meticulous and unlikely as Chinese farmers' terraces.

Above all, of course, there are the roads. From the few Roman roads, through Chesterton's Saxon drunkard's roads ('A reeling road, a rolling road, that rambles round the shire'), right up to the motorways, those great earthworks driven out of London from the 1960s which have redefined and redrawn England as dramatically as the stark cathedrals and castles of the Norman Conquest. They have their grandeur too, and the most complicated junctions – knotted like a sailor's demonstration – are beautiful.

For me, this endless scoring, gouging and cross-hatching is far more representative of England than any building, however fine, or mists, or even the birds and animals who are constantly moving on, and coming in, because of climate change. (My local park is all screech and apple green – the parakeets have taken over.) All round the world, landscapes are wilting, drying out and being emptied of variety by human activity. What makes England special is that here the lines are rarely signs of neglect or surrender. They are signs of husbandry, ownership, old mistakes healing and wealth taken in scores of ways without disaster.

Lines in time remind us that even the ugliest places mend. There are forests hiding the mess of the iron industry in the Sussex Weald; hauntingly dramatic mining quarries, long abandoned, in Lancashire; and the splintered, claggy remnants of Cornish tin-mining used to lure tourists. Lovely remote lakes turn out to be reservoirs, concealing drowned villages; spreading Georgian parkland hides the secret of the farms demolished to make it 'wild'. Nothing is for ever and nothing is what it seems.

Thus, nothing is hopeless either. The lines are drawn, rubbed out and drawn again. No line is final. These are not lines of beauty, but lines of experience and compromise.

This takes me to the final line, an echo of all that, which is simply the line of the quizzical English smile – that off-centre, knowing, half-smile you find on so many faces. The Alan Bennett, David Hockney, Beryl Bainbridge, Judi Dench smile which says, 'Been here a while, seen quite a lot, not so easy to fool, still learning.' In this land of lines, it's the line that underlines how hard the English are to really know.

SCOURING THE COUNTRYSIDE

Peter Marren
on white horses

Is it really a horse? The famous figure carved out of the chalk on the downs at Uffington, Oxfordshire, has been known as the White Horse for a thousand years, though to my eyes it's a dead ringer for a fox. But whatever it is, the villagers liked it. Every so often they would wander up the hill and pick the outline clean so that it gleamed from afar like fresh snow melting in the sun. These ritual 'scourings' were part of a jolly day out, as Uffington's most famous local, Thomas Hughes, author of *Tom Brown's Schooldays*, recorded in verse in 1859:

> *There'll be backsword play and climmin' the powl,*
> *And a race for a pig and a cheese;*
> *And us thinks as hisns a dummel soul*
> *As dwoan't care for zich spwoarts as these.*

Scouring was a custom dating back, some say, to the days of King Alfred, who was said to have trounced the Danes hereabouts (hence the 'backsword play'). Yet having a well-weeded White Horse on the doorstep never seemed to benefit any of the dedicated locals since, remarkably, they couldn't actually see it. In fact, even today it's hard to make out from the ground. Depending on your viewpoint, it is not so much a horse as a collection of chalky slivers or letters from some Kabbalistic alphabet.

Only from the air can you enjoy what Mary Delorme calls its 'soaring rapture'. And that is surely the point. Whoever originally cut the figure in the virgin turf of the Uffington Downs – and the latest evidence suggests it was done around three thousand years ago – deliberately chose a line near the top, the least visible part of a convex slope. Clearly, it was not intended for human eyes. Like those mysterious lines in the Peruvian desert, it was made for the celestial gaze of a sky god.

Perhaps that is why the creature seems to us less like a depiction of an earth-bound horse and more like a spirit of some kind, half-running, half-flying across the down. Celtic art drew from nature without being tied to a literal rendition of form, and I imagine sky gods might have appreciated a bit of human imagination. And so some prehistoric genius produced something wholly startling; not so much an animal as a lithe spirit of grace and freedom; not so much an assertion as a gift.

Move on 2,700 years and we find another collection of white shapes on the downs of my home county, Wiltshire. No ambivalence this time: these are real horses with prancing legs, clodhopping feet and pricked ears. Nor are they half-hidden from view, but carved where they can be seen for miles. The best of them, in Pewsey Vale, was designed by journeyman painter Jack Thorn, who was paid twenty golden sovereigns for his trouble. (Later on, we learn, Jack Thorn was hanged for 'a variety of crimes'.) The next best, at Westbury, stands stock still as if made of concrete; which, in fact, it is – concrete having been poured over the chalk to deter weeds. And the small one at Preshute is a joke. It was cut by Marlborough schoolboys in 1805 and has what some say is an extra leg – although I can't say that's what it looks like.

Unlike the Uffington animal, these naively rendered horses, hacked out of the chalk at the whim of the local farmer, are exactly what you'd expect – mere cut-outs. Yet, when three were allowed to disappear (and a fourth ploughed up), we missed them. Perhaps we sense in them the freedom and joy of galloping on the wild, open downs with the wind in our hair. They are happy horses, forever prancing with the skylarks and bees. Perhaps they embody a wish that life itself could be like that.

THE SECRET KINGDOM OF MARROWLAND

Simon Sebag Montefiore

on marrows

Empires and kingdoms rise and fall in the English countryside just as they do in the histories of nations and conquerors. Some are famous: the deer that rule some glen or wood; the hares that leap across the fields, the owl that dominates his tree, the fox that rules that field, the avenue of oaks that stand like guards, even the bluebells that rule the forest for a few gorgeously purple days . . . Some are less obvious and less known, but they can be celebrated too. Marrows have become more than a vegetable to us, they have become a way of life, a religion, a kingdom, a holy grail, they have become the summer.

Each year my children and I plant the marrow seeds in the same place, and each year their luxuriant green plants, with their wide, rough, dusty leaves, their slightly prickly stems, their far-reaching tendrils and, of course, their fat, fecund, bulbous, obscene, generous vegetables take over this corner of the countryside. The marrows are greedy and invincible; nothing seems to eat them, even the rabbits and pheasants and pigeons that eat everything else all around them, but they themselves rise up and then conquer, their tendrils sometimes reaching ten feet from their home base. There is something exotic and uninhibited about them in the way of few other vegetables. They go wild in the country.

Marrows are often disdained, yet their flesh is no more tasteless than broccoli or spinach, their fruits are infinitely more lush and magnificent, and once planted they become part of the forest and the hedges – rather like wild blackberries or wild rhubarb. They have become the very embodiment of the joy of the countryside in the English summer for my two children, who check on them every day. Each child has its own marrows. First, crouching on all fours, they peer under the wide leaves and point out the bright-yellow flowers. Then, when they spot the first marrows, there are decisions to make: to pick and fry as courgettes or to leave and let them grow as huge as possible. Soon they have taken over everything and then the children announce that we are living in Marrowland, a new kingdom in which the marrow reigns for the summer. They return to us with handfuls of courgettes and we fry them for tea.

Meanwhile, the children report each day on the size and colouring of the ever-increasing marrows. Each one is different, growing in a unique shape and colour: there are the stripy ones, the dark-green ones, the yellow zucchinis. Like people, these marrows get tanned, but when they are picked, they are pale underneath as if wearing a bikini. Some are large and the children excitedly slice them open and cut out the seeds and roast them; others are so huge that they have a life and character of their own and must be kept. The children name each of these huge marrows Monty, and number and describe them like kings: Monty IV, the Great, or Monty II, the Bulbous.

There are yelps of pleasure when a hidden marrow, growing unnoticed under some dusty old leaf, is suddenly discovered in its embarrassing enormity. All around our cottage marrows laze, comfortable in their size and glory.

Finally, in October, the marrow bushes start to shrivel and finally die. The fat marrows, even the King Montys, go soft, or we roast them. And then it's winter and we return to normal life. Marrowland vanishes as if it had never existed. Until next year.

FAIR PLAY

Brian Moore
on sports fields

THEY STAND OUT DO sports fields; regulation-sized bits of turf set on valley floors or perched impossibly on the only near-level land for miles around, they often appear in the least likely of places.

All of us have at some time seen a golf course that blended into the contours of its surroundings or the small triangles or H-shaped goalposts which served to mark the goal of a succession of games. We have heard cries of 'goal' and 'howzat' echoing in the distance as we have tried to picture games being played and points scored. Was the scorer an athletic youth, or an ageing father whose shirt barely covered up his growing girth?

Sometimes these sports fields show up as the only natural feature in seemingly endless swathes of continuous concrete which deadens the senses, reducing everything to a dull grey. Even when run-down and tatty these open spaces encourage social exchange, team building and competition, promoting values often at odds with their surroundings.

Impossible longings for summer evenings of cricket on the village green fill many descriptions of what England was and should be; that these often never really existed does not matter, because it is their essence, not their existence, that is important.

It is true that you can still find idyllic ovals here and there, perfectly manicured and loved. Although most are not enclosed by magnificent stands, nor surrounded by thousands of supporters, each sports field is worth preserving because thereon ordinary people play out extraordinary dreams of triumph. They allow us to try and emulate our heroes' deeds, feats and victories.

Sports fields are needed now more than ever, because they offer so much that makes us better. Successive promises by politicians that sports fields are safe in their hands have proved worthless, and their disingenuousness is not only foolhardy, it is destructive.

It is not just the disappearance of visually attractive green spaces that matters when we lose another sports field, though that in itself is of huge regret; it is all that goes with it that is lost.

Camaraderie through sport creates lasting friendships. Working as a team for a greater good can curb destructive individualism, and prepare young people for life's inevitable setbacks and losses. Our general health is improved by physical exertion, and with it our state of mind. On our sports fields there are no barriers of class, race or wealth, each person is set free to compete on equal terms, to challenge themselves to give of their best without having to contend with prejudices over which they have no control.

Perhaps it is because sports fields are not seen as 'countryside' that they are not regarded as being as important and worth saving as areas of natural beauty.

However, given all the benefits that stem from them we must fight to preserve them as much as any special view or endangered wood or river.

These fields of sporting endeavour take us beyond the present and create memories of contests past and matches still to come. The winning run, the final goal and the flowing try live on in the minds of the players and spectators, and so with the aesthetic come the athletic memories that do not dim. Sports fields have always been part of us, and must continue to be valued as an important asset of England.

AN ENDURING
AFFAIR

Richard Muir
on Nidderdale and history

WHY WAS IT THAT lads of the 1950s – we ramblers through nettle-, bramble- and thistle-infested countrysides – were always clad in shorts? I can picture myself in shorts of brown corduroy, with a windjammer to match. I am out in the hollowed lanes, following riverside tracks where only anglers should go, or cutting across country along the branch line, where I certainly should not have been. A border collie, sometimes two of them, would also figure in the scene.

As I roamed in that Yorkshire dale I was forever aware of heaviness in the air and a tense ache inside. It was the burden of history. I could feel the past encroaching with every breath and step, and shimmering in every wall, track, farmstead or hedgerow. It seemed like the ghosts of old Nidderdale – Cistercian monks, legionaries on the move or stooped lead miners – were tugging at my shoulders or whispering in a gibberish I could not comprehend.

History did not feature much in the affairs of the village school, where most time was devoted to rehearsals for the Christmas concert. One day, however, we learned about a Dr Raistrick, who 'discovered ancient objects'. (This was Arthur Raistrick, geologist, archaeologist and the remarkable biographer of the Dales landscape, who inspired cohorts of followers and revealed his personal courage when interned as a pacifist during the First World War.) Knowing nothing of academic doctorates, I imagined that Dr Raistrick – plainly a keen-eyed fellow – must spot his ancient objects when out doing the rounds of his patients in a pony and trap. I added a little colour to my supposition by imagining that, every so often, these spectacular objects would be displayed to an admiring audience in Harrogate's Royal Hall. Though my interpretation was unsound, I had, in realizing that countryside places and features have histories that can be studied, passed an important milestone.

My escalating infatuation with the rural landscape proved a bad preparation for a career based on studying historic landscape. Having miraculously passed my eleven-plus, I found myself a yokel and bumpkin among the urbane achievers of the grammar school. Never having encountered a decimal point in the village school, I would have no truck with them thereafter (O Level maths: twenty-five per cent). My bike was always waiting by the village store, so I could leap from school bus to bike and then charge for the fields in a blur of pedals and flying grit. No number of detentions could divert me from village cricket or the school's teams, and I can never recall doing any homework – certainly not during daylight hours, anyway.

The countryside has remained my haven, my challenge and my sweetheart. Since the coming of the mobile phone, my love of travel has become a dread. But I still get more excited at the prospect of arriving and encountering new countrysides than I ever have before. There is an old pop song by the Teddy Bears proclaiming that to know him was to love him. I believe that the better one knows the countryside – its evolution, its lost communities and its history – then the more one will love it.

MY CORNER SHOP

Daljit Nagra
on local stores

NAPOLEON ONCE MOCKINGLY DESCRIBED Britain as a nation of shopkeepers. And in many ways, when I consider the corner shops from my childhood, I think he was right. These shops were neatly ordered establishments. They pleased the eye as much as they displeased the pocket. They were convenience stores that were rarely convenient.

My parents often worked overtime at a factory, so if we ever fancied a dessert of tinned fruit cocktail with Carnation Evaporated Milk, the corner shop at the end of our road would certainly be shut. In fact, as I recall, it used to shut at 5 p.m. on weekdays, with a half-day opening on Saturdays, and was closed all day Sunday. There were frequent impromptu tea breaks (when a placard would be strung up saying 'Back in a minute'), and one-hour breaks for lunch.

The corner shop I revere is the Indian type that sprang up around the country from the late 1970s. The owners worked on the principle that shops should be emporia, and set about fulfilling this macro-ambition despite the shortage of spaces, cheerily ignoring the logic that says things should be easy to find and to reach if you expect people to buy them.

In 1982, my parents bought a shop in Sheffield. The first thing we did was increase the opening hours to a simple numeric of 9 a.m. to 9 p.m., every day of the week – with no sneaky tea or lunch breaks. It had been the kind of store that sold basic groceries, cigarettes and fresh bread from one bakery. But we soon had bread delivered from three bakeries to extend the choice; a video-loan service;

bouquets of flowers; daily copies of the Sheffield newspaper, *The Star*; a fresh fruit and veg corner; a broken-biscuit discount rack; stacks of 55lb sacks of potatoes; two deep freezers; a wide range of dairy produce in open-shelved fridges and, best of all, we obtained an off-licence and sold alcohol. We would have incorporated a postal service but, sadly, there was a post office in the area (which kept to the old British opening hours that left locals moaning in our shop . . .).

Our shop was like most Indian corner shops. We sold everything we could and packed it all in, on the simple principle of 'anything goes'. Sure enough, anything did go, and while I rarely knew where things were (mops would sometimes be found alongside the video display and a stack of pink biscuits would peer from the crisps area), this approach seemed to encourage the customers to look harder, so they would end up purchasing things they didn't even know they had wanted.

Despite the threat from supermarkets that seem to never, ever close, I am sure the corner shop will survive because people will always appreciate the local touch. After all, where else is a brief chat about the weather all part of the service?

ANCIENT JEWELS

John Julius Norwich
on village churches

LOOK AT ANY OF those old travel posters – for the railways, perhaps, or for Shell – or the jackets of those lovely Batsford guidebooks, and there you will see it: the quintessential English village, nestling in a fold of the hills, with the church at its heart. More often than not, the church will have a spire – a relative rarity unless we happen to be in Northamptonshire – but who cares? The point has been made: no other building, not the manor house, not the market cross, not the war memorial, can hope to take the place of the church as the central focus of the community.

It will be far older than any of them, for a start. It might easily go back to the eleventh century; the church at Bradwell in Essex is four centuries older still. In all too many, the Victorian restorers have done their worst – Gilbert Scott, in particular, has a lot to answer for – but several thousand have, thank God, remained essentially unspoilt, a collection of historical and architectural jewels that no other country can begin to match.

Today's church crawlers, however, face a problem unknown to their grandparents. Until the 1950s or there-abouts, village churches were always open in daylight hours: today, alas, where there is thought to be a risk of robbery or vandalism, the casual visitor may arrive to discover the door firmly locked against him. He should accept this philosophically, provided only that there is a notice in the porch informing him where the key may be obtained.

Were I a bishop, I should insist not only on such notices, but also on the proper disposition of the electric light switches inside the building. How often does one arrive at a small parish church on a November afternoon, only for one's relief at finding the door unlocked to change to frustration at the impossibility of seeing anything at all amid the encircling gloom – a frustration increased by the knowledge that the switches have almost certainly been hidden on purpose, presumably to prevent wastage of electricity. Experience, admittedly, gradually reveals the usual hiding places: try looking behind the chancel or tower arches, inside the vestry or beside the organ.

But why will parish councils not install coin machines, which – at a deliberately inflated price – will flood the building with light for five minutes or so and then automatically switch themselves off? Until they do, we must continue to arm ourselves with the most powerful torch we can find, and never stir without it.

Experience also brings expertise. It goes without saying that the more we know about churches, the more we shall enjoy them. There are two essential books on the subject that no respectable crawler should be without. The first – long out of print, but I am sure obtainable from Amazon – is *The Parish Church as a Work of Art* by the much-lamented Alec Clifton-Taylor. No one ever knew as much about the subject as he did; he made long and detailed notes of every church he visited, revising them when he returned, perhaps thirty or forty years later. Virtually everything I know on the subject I owe to him.

The second is *England's Thousand Best Churches*, by Simon Jenkins. This too is an astonishing achievement. A frighteningly busy and hugely prolific journalist, now Chairman of the National Trust, he has somehow found the time to travel the length and breadth of the country, not only visiting the churches but thinking long and hard about them and describing them unforgettably.

With these two volumes safely tucked in the glove compartment, you will need no other. And what delights lie in store . . .

THE POINT OF NO RETURN

Sean O'Brien
on Spurn Point

EAST YORKSHIRE IS A little-known part of England. East of Hull – a city of three hundred thousand – rich arable farmlands stretch to the North Sea, which is rapidly reclaiming much of the coast. It's a place of silence; somewhere history seems to have finished with. The land narrows southwards past a heavily secured gas depot and a mysterious MoD museum, and then the sea and the Humber Estuary converge, and you're heading down to Spurn Point – the boom of the sea to one side, the quiet of the mudflats to the other. You're here, wherever 'here' is.

Spurn Point is a narrow, curving landspit of sand, shingle and low grassy dunes. It's a RSPB sanctuary and home to England's only full-time lifeboat crew and their families. The Humber river pilots have their dock here. Beyond the huddle of lifeboatmen's houses, a wood of hawthorns masks old gun emplacements. It feels like the end of the world – which is why, I think, as children we liked it so much. To travel there in the old red bus from Hull Central Library was like going to the draughty doorway of the world and looking through. You could see the jolt where the North Sea and the Humber met, and the old fort at Bull Island, the ships sliding in and out – and beyond it all, a vast emptiness under the grey-white weather of childhood.

You can still see these things, but Spurn Head is changing. The locals don't like it when people say that high tides breach the landspit. They prefer the phrase 'washed over', as though language itself is a defence against rising sea levels. The last time I was there – last autumn – Spurn had just been washed over. A section of shingle and sand had been shipped off elsewhere and a section of the road had been shunted thirty yards west. Visitors had to walk the last mile. Two workmen were repairing the road with flexible nets of concrete laid down like engineering Elastoplast. They knew they'd be back soon. They, too, love the place, quite aside from making a living there.

At some time, though, someone will make a decision on economic grounds that the place is beyond saving. The sea means to have Spurn, like most of East Yorkshire – which is, after all, merely the 12,000-year-old detritus left by the last Ice Age. The sea will take back Sunk Island, that chill and eerie stretch of hard-won farmland just inland from Spurn. It will revisit Hull, which was disastrously flooded in 2007. And at some point, not too far off, it will not go away again. W. H. Auden said that poets love scenes of disaster, and I understand what he meant – the challenge of a big set piece; the wreck of the fleet or an army gone under the sand. But what he didn't mention was that it helps to have somewhere to stand and witness or imagine the catastrophe. When the ground is gone from under your feet, the poet's role changes from observer to elegist. Spurn Point will see me out, but others will not be so lucky. Go there if you can, before it's too late.

LIVING ON THE EDGE

Michael Palin

on crags

I WAS BORN AND brought up in Sheffield. In the 1950s, before the ascendancy of her near neighbour, Leeds, Sheffield was the fourth largest city in England. Some half a million people were squeezed into her hills and valleys, and a pall of pollution from a succession of huge steel foundries smothered the long rows of back-to-back houses on the east side of the city.

I was unequivocally a city boy. My father worked in the heart of the steel-producing district. The shops, schools and cinemas that marked my territorial bounds were all to the east, drawing me back into the city. But there was one exception. Somewhere, not far from my home, where nature still ruled, a young boy could have great dreams. He could see, in their pristine state, the valleys and rivers that had driven the mills and the forges that had made Sheffield famous. The very word for this place was evocative of something strong and uncompromising, like Sheffielders themselves: crags.

The approach to the crags was suitably difficult, but for the most banal of reasons. They were accessed via a public footpath across a private golf course. I think my general, non-specific dislike of clubs and those who join them was certainly strengthened, if not originally founded, by having to creep across the fairway with the warning shouts of the privileged ringing in my ears. Once safely across the course, a tall iron-barred gate gave way to a rocky path, which for a while clung claustrophobically to the side of a formidable stone wall. As the darkened wings in a theatre lead out on to the space and light of the stage, so this uneven, awkward little trail opened quite suddenly on to the edge of the earth and the sky.

It was as abrupt and epic a transformation from city to country as you could imagine. There were no fences, no restraints and, provided your father wasn't looking, you could shuffle, stomach churning, to the very end of the land, where sharp-cut parapets of millstone grit teased us towards the abyss. Far down below – or so it seemed to a schoolboy – tiny vehicles swished along the A57. Below that, glimpsed between a line of trees and bushes, ran the tiny Rivelin, a stream now, but one that had cut this valley over millions of years. And across the river, rose our sister slope – one very different from ours, not jagged and precipitous but broad and benign – dotted with sturdy farmhouses and green fields partitioned by dry-stone walls.

It was a cracker of a view. To the west, the road wound its way towards Manchester, eventually disappearing as the valley narrowed and climbed towards the Pennine foothills. To the east, you might, on a rare clear day, catch sight of the dark satanic mills of the steelworks. Such a confluence of man and nature could coax the romantic out of anyone.

When I was old enough to go up to the crags by myself, I'd walk along the sandy, precipitous paths with my imagination romping ahead of me – taking me to the Wild West, the Grand Canyon or the Lost World. As I grew older, my father increasingly deferred to the quieter countryside of his native East Anglia. Here I saw the sea for the first time, churches made of flint and the spooky reedbeds of the Norfolk Broads. Lovely country, but for one who had passed through that metal gate at the end of the golf course, it was pretty tame stuff. When I hear Elgar, it's not East Anglia I imagine, but the inimitable grandeur of the crags that loom over the Rivelin Valley.

TAKING ROOT

Jonathon Porritt
on stand-alone trees

WHEN I WAS AT Oxford University in the early 1970s, I lived outside the city for a year, in a place called Boars Hill. Being somewhat disaffected with Oxford at that time, I rarely went into the centre and managed to keep tutors and others happy from afar. As a result, I got to know the surrounding countryside extremely well, with many long walks – and even more short walks en route to the local pub!

The footpath involved in that particular excursion ran alongside a huge field – farming in Oxfordshire was being fully intensified at that time, with average field size increasing year on year. In the middle of this field stood a large but not particularly beautiful oak tree, apparently in good health and very hard to ignore. It's difficult to explain now, but that tree adopted me during the course of that year; and ever since I have been an absolute sucker for solitary mature trees in cultivated fields.

You would be amazed how many there are once you start looking for them. But what are they doing there? A landowner, however many years ago, must have consciously decided to leave that tree totally untouched – perhaps to provide shelter for livestock in fields that had been used for grazing before being converted to arable farming? Or just because? And every one of that farmer's heirs must have consciously decided that was the way things should stay.

It's hard to think of a more eloquent snook being cocked at the iron-clad laws of economic efficiency. Every square inch that tree takes up is a square inch not devoted to profit maximization. Every bit of goodness that tree sucks up through its roots is goodness and water lost to a particular crop. Every outing of the drill or plough or harvester will be irritatingly inconvenienced by having to deviate around its immovable presence. By that measure, the more barren and prairie-like the farmed landscape, the more powerful a statement such stand-alones seem to make.

Of course they do provide a return, but in metrics that are currently dangerously devalued. Such trees (particularly oaks) are often host to all sorts of benign predators that help control pest infestations in the surrounding crop – vertical beetle banks, if you like, sustaining an enclave of biodiversity in a monocultural desert. And as far as the local community is concerned, such trees provide continuity and constancy, a small but telling riposte to those who say that the only thing that never changes is change itself.

I only watched my Boars Hill oak through one set of seasonal shifts, but even now I can recall the observance of detail, colour, density and transparency. And that's the same rhythm – year in, year out – without surprises. I am what I am, such a tree says, so relate to me on my own terms. When I returned, years later, the tree was still there, and although the immediate continuity was broken, the connection continued. Whenever I see trees like these, I feel they are waiting for us to get our act together, pre-eminent *genii loci*, anticipating the day we humans finally rediscover what it is to be at one with the natural world. Possibly not in my lifetime – but I have no doubt these resolute survivors are somehow telling us that we shouldn't leave it too much longer.

WHATEVER THE WEATHER

Gavin Pretor-Pinney
on clouds

SAMUEL JOHNSON WAS ALWAYS one for observation. 'It is commonly observed,' he once wrote, 'that when two Englishmen meet, their first talk is of the weather.' This is still true today, though it is perhaps less remarkable: with the uncertainties of climate change, you can probably say the same about most nationalities.

Some claim that our love of discussing the weather stems from a social unease – that debating the chances of rain before tea merely serves to deflect attention from less anodyne matters. This is a very clichéd and outdated image of the English. The fact of the matter is that we have a lot to say about the English weather because there is a lot of it going on.

The British Isles inhabit latitudes where warm tropical air and cold polar air battle for supremacy, the North Atlantic being their favourite zone of conflict. England is one of the first in line to receive these meteorological skirmishes as they head west. But our island position, in close proximity to the warm waters of the Gulf Stream, also ensures that our winters are much milder than elsewhere at equivalent latitudes.

The unpredictability of the English weather seems, inevitably, to turn our discussions into moans: it is too damp, too cold, too cloudy . . . Yet the wild, changing, seasonal glory of our weather has shaped the beautiful English countryside. Why do so many of us yearn for the clear blue skies of California, Spain or Australia? They seem to represent, in our collective mind's eye, not just an idea of paradise, but nostalgia for the endless and cloudless summer days of our childhood. We dismiss clouds; they are brutish harbingers of bad weather and bad times. This attitude has even infiltrated our language. We talk in a derogatory way about someone with their 'head in the clouds', or shiver with a sense of foreboding at the prospect of a 'cloud on the horizon'. 'Blue-sky thinking', on the other hand, has more positive connotations.

This is a form of madness. Why must we continue to believe the grass is greener where the skies are relentlessly blue? The English weather has sculpted the contours of our uplands and nourished the mossy woodlands of our valleys; it is as varied as the landscape itself. There is nothing more exquisite than a soft warm day in early May when the hawthorn is heavy with blossom and the grass a lush green from winter rains. What can match the invigorating howl of an autumn gale (especially when you are tucked up warm inside)? Or the muffled crunch of footsteps on a winter morning when the world lies a foot deep in fresh snow?

The clouds of England are not just rain-filled annoyances. They bring beauty to our sunsets, nourishment to our gardens and ever-changing airy sculptures to our skies. Our clouds are ethereal, majestic works of art that are also the most egalitarian of nature's displays, available to us all. Everyone has a ringside seat and you don't have to live in an area of outstanding beauty to appreciate them.

The Victorian critic John Ruskin said, 'For me, nothing has ever rivalled the variety and drama of clouds.' These free displays of abstract art, so much a part of the English climate, are something to be celebrated.

HOLDING BACK
THE SEA

Libby Purves
on harbour walls

GIVE THANKS AND PRAISE for harbour walls. This is a rugged island, and though it has some fine natural harbours guarded by rocks, especially in the west, it is the unsung industry of generations which has made our coast safe for the sailor. Quays and breakwaters, stone and cement, artful shapes devised with local cunning to hold away the storms and swells: these are not just picturesque. To those who will listen, their stones sing of patient ingenuity and heroic carefulness; a quiet legacy from a harder-working age.

For the casual stroller, a stone pier or seaward promenade is merely a convenient bit of scenery: mossy, salty, a place to admire fishing boats and defy the waves. You sit of an evening on a worn old bollard, and hardly recognize how brilliantly placed a warping point it was, for turning the old sailing ships before the age of power.

For the sailor, taking a small boat round the coast, the old harbours spell safety and rest. Look down from the heights of Whitby towards the gallant bulwarks of Whitby harbour, see the cobles chugging in, dodging the shifting banks where the Esk deposits its silt; see the tide go out in Bridlington, and the police horses exercising on the hard sand between the piers. Or look at the curled beauty of Charlestown, the pier at St Ives, the clever basin at Ramsgate, the granite walls of Aberdeen or the rounded masonry of Portpatrick: and as you look, think of their maker John Smeaton, the eighteenth-century genius who was the first modern civil engineer, and who understood the power of water and the needs of boatmen as fully as he knew his materials.

The west is magnificent; but to me it is the east coast harbours which are most moving. They speak of the eternal, humble give-and-take of humanity with the sea: of reaching out into the unknown and hoping for the homecoming. There is something gallant about these little sandy harbours, assisted by few natural features: they have crept seawards, not with the arrogance of the great industrial shipyards but with persistent local determination to defy disaster, raise the money, catch fish, take trade, and give insignificant out-of-the-way towns a maritime back door and an identity with the world. Praise them.

DIG FOR VICTORY

Tony Robinson
on Mick Aston

BEFORE I MET MICK Aston, I thought archaeology was all about treasure hunting, and that an archaeologist's job involved digging enthusiastically into hillsides, and pulling out skulls and rusty swords. But under his tutelage, my eyes were opened to the fact that our archaeological heritage is an invaluable and irreplaceable part of our landscape – one that should be treated with love and respect.

One frosty morning, early in our friendship, he took me to the top of a church tower in the Welsh Marches. Below us was Much Wenlock, a typical little country town like so many others; the sort of place you'd stop off at to have a trawl round the gift shops, then drive on until you found a pretty country pub with an interesting lunch menu.

But Mick showed me a version of Much Wenlock that the casual tourist never sees. It was what he called 'the palimpsest of history' – the way the modern buildings overlaid the Georgian town, which cut through the Tudor plots that lie on top of the Norman street pattern, which itself surrounded a Saxon monastery. He pointed out how the tangle of streets and alleyways had a ruthless logic to them, how each one represented the needs of a particular group of people at a particular time in the settlement's history.

I could see why the town was built where it is, adjacent to a ford and at the head of a valley – the route between Wales and England for millennia. And beyond all this, I saw that what had initially seemed like a vague jumble of fields and hills were, in fact, medieval field systems, abandoned quarries and fishponds, prehistoric burial grounds and Roman trackways.

The English landscape and its archaeology are under threat as never before from deep ploughing, inappropriate legislation, irresponsible metal detecting, theft, global warming and general ignorance. Mick Aston is a quirky, wise and Rabelaisian champion of our countryside who has inspired a generation of archaeologists (and armchair archaeologists) to look at our landscape as a portrait of change. It is a portrait we must cherish for the sake of future generations. I just wish there were more like him.

SMILING AT THE NEIGHBOURS

Alexei Sayle
on rural friendliness

In 1984, WITH THE money I made from a hit single, I bought a small house in a village in rural Northamptonshire. I'd been performing the song on *Top of the Pops* the week before we moved in, and a kid in the village told me that his gran had watched the programme knowing somebody on it was buying Manor Cottage. 'As long as it's not that fat one in the tight suit, I don't mind who it is,' she'd said.

Our house had a paddock planted with an amazing variety of vegetables by the previous owner, and I was standing in front of a row of carrots wondering how I could use the grass rake I was holding to get them up, when a man started talking to me from the churchyard which adjoined our land. I thought I was prepared for all the unsettling things about the countryside, the silence followed by the sound of things killing other things, the different kinds of trees, the emptiness, the dazzling colours of the wild flowers, but what I hadn't expected was the friendliness. In London nobody talks to you outside the house – your parents would ignore you if you were in the same Tube carriage together – so I was so thrown by a man I didn't know talking to me that I flung down the rake and ran inside the house without saying a word.

The next day, my wife and I were walking down a lane when a woman coming towards us wished us a cheery good morning. 'What's she after?' I asked my wife once the woman was out of earshot. My wife explained that the woman wasn't after anything, she wasn't planning to rob me or sell me insurance, she was just being friendly for the sake of it, as people in the country were. My wife also said that if I was going to live in the country, I was going to have to learn to be friendly too. This was an entirely new concept for me, but I decided to take it on board. The following day I went for a walk by myself along a disused railway line that ran through the countryside behind our house, determined to try rural friendliness. After about half an hour I came upon a man who was tending a goat that he kept in a sort of lean-to on the other side of the hedge. I strode up to him and with a big smile on my face shouted at him, 'Nice goat!' I felt like I was making progress.

PARADISE FOUND

John Sergeant
on Great Tew

THERE ARE SO MANY wonderful villages in England that to pick out one to represent all is clearly unreasonable. But for someone brought up in Great Tew in Oxfordshire, the choice is easy. It is the perfect example of a model seventeenth-century village estate, with its honey-coloured thatched cottages, its Norman church and splendid pub, the famous Falkland Arms. During my formative years I came to know it as only a child does, with a close knowledge of every fold of the hills, every tree and almost every bush.

In the 1950s, for a small boy interested in climbing trees, setting up camp and shooting at birds with a catapult, Great Tew was paradise. But I could not be as wild as I would have liked because my father was the vicar. In church, we – my brother, sister and I – had to stay for his sermons, while the other children were allowed to leave early. One glorious Sunday, I remember walking through the snow to find that no one else had managed to attend. The church was empty. I was convinced my father would press on regardless, but he read out a single prayer and we were released. I vividly remember that happy day, throwing snowballs and playing with our toboggan in the soft yellow light of a winter sun.

In this Cotswold village, modern life was kept at bay. All three of us went to the primary school on the village green, an easy walk down the hill from home. There was an impressive teacher, Mrs Bury, who lived to see the twenty-first century, dying at the age of one hundred. She taught her thirty pupils in a large schoolroom. We would sit in six rows of desks and we moved up a row at the end of each year. Only rarely did we see a television, and even the stocks on the village green were kept in working order to remind potential miscreants of how they might have been treated in the bad old days.

Our main local town was Oxford. There was a bus once a week, but our family – one of the lucky ones – owned a car and my parents would sometimes take us if, as they later admitted, we were being more of a nuisance than usual. I was only thirteen when we left the Georgian vicarage – just opposite the entrance to the church – for the last time. At that age, it took me a long time to get over the fact that most people did not live in such idyllic surroundings.

Great Tew has changed a lot since I was a boy. It is far more prosperous. Many of the houses which in the past could only be rented by people who worked on the estate – for the miserly sum of £2 a year – have now been sold. Some of the new owners spend their working week in London. In many ways the place has come out of its time warp. But it would still be an obvious contender for the title given to it by a magazine more than sixty years ago: the prettiest village in Britain.

THE BARD'S OWN RIVER

Antony Sher
on the Avon

WE LIVE IN STRATFORD-UPON-AVON for at least half the year; my partner, Greg Doran, works for the Royal Shakespeare Company as Chief Associate Director, and much of my acting career has been spent with them too. We're lucky. Our apartment is situated right on the Avon. On bright mornings you wake to what looks like a biblical spectacle, causing you to cup your hands over your eyes – the water is ablaze with sunshine, and reflections are playing on the walls and ceilings around you. Swans float or fly by, Canada geese, a heron, the electric-blue glint of a kingfisher. And, in early summer, noisy mobs of seagulls. The eels have arrived. These extraordinary creatures are spawned in the Sargasso Sea, south of Bermuda; they cross the Atlantic to British waters, enter the Severn Estuary, take a right into the Avon at Tewkesbury, progress to Stratford, wriggle up a specially built ramp, the Eel Ladder, on the weir at Lucy's Mill, and then those who have survived Atlantic perils and Stratford seagulls, finally mate. They then turn round and start on the four thousand mile journey back. Nature must have been drunk when she made them.

Before breakfast, we go for a walk. Within minutes we're on a rough path on the north bank, a stretch known as Seven Meadows, where the spire of Trinity Church quickly retreats into the distance. It never fails to inspire me: the sudden openness of the land, the yellow-brown glow of the river, the tall black shade of the woods opposite. In little clearings at the water's edge, lone fishermen sit, lost in meditation. I'm from South Africa, and English terrain will always be vaguely unfamiliar, so I rejoice in the fact that

Greg (raised in Yorkshire) treats these expeditions as nature trails. 'Look at all the butterflies today,' he'll say. 'These are cabbage whites, these red admirals, and this – watch as it opens its wings – a peacock.' We reach the last meadow, Greg's favourite, profusely overgrown with wild flowers: 'Here's the burdock that Lear makes into a crown, here are the long purples that Ophelia weaves into her garland.'

Of course – it hits you again and again – this is where Shakespeare grew up, these are the first things he saw and heard and smelled.

Just after Stanals Bridge we cross to the other bank for our return. Here the views are more spectacular. You're high above the river to your left, and to your right the horizon is high above you. The world feels tilted, marvellously, yet somehow everything is still upright, whether the holiday barges passing below, with flower pots on their roofs and bemused dogs at their helms, or the farm workers on the field which slopes up to the sky; they're harvesting a pea crop, speaking to one another in Polish, their voices echoing slightly in the clear morning air.

'Look,' says Greg. 'That wren is so small, yet his call is so loud.' We watch a fisherman catch a tench. Greg smiles. 'See the small red spots on its scales. In *Henry IV Part I*, a traveller complains about the fleas in his inn: "I am stung like a tench!"'

The walk lasts exactly an hour. At the end, you feel like you've taken some magic tonic – Essence of Shakespeare, maybe – setting you up for the day's work ahead.

When we're based back in London, I don't know how I do without it.

IN DEFENCE OF TOTNES

Lucy Siegle
on Totnes Castle

GIRLS, IF YOU WANT to start an argument with a boy, try taking said male to Totnes Castle. 'Actually, this is a motte and bailey structure,' my paramour will say, finessing my blunt usage of 'castle'. This is because he spent too much time reading *Asterix*. 'Why does it say "Castle" on the sign then?' I reply. And so it continues.

Granted, it is not a castle in the Caerphilly or Caernarfon sense of the word. Those Welsh versions verge on Disney, with lots of turrets and outposts. Totnes, meanwhile, is a rather straightforward circular keep with some impressive wooden doors. Those Normans didn't mess about with architectural flourishes. Unlike Glastonbury Tor – where, in order to get the full effect, you have to use your imagination to envision the plains below flooded – Totnes has no pretensions. It is the WYSIWYG (what-you-see-is-what-you-get) of the castle community. And it is perfectly possible to soak up its vibes without any imagination at all.

Vibes are very important in Totnes, which has more than its fair share of crystal shops; more than anybody's fair share, in fact. The castle – presumably constructed originally for bellicose reasons – these days gives positive vibes. It is accepting, gender-unspecific (I normally think of castles as being male), and provides the perfect acoustic for playing a didgeridoo (there are many of these in Totnes).

To be quite honest, nobody really makes a fuss about the castle; and that in itself is quintessentially Totnesian. For years the youth of Totnes (a demographic that once involved me) have traipsed around the neat grass inside the circular perimeters getting up to no good. The castle, therefore, forms nothing more than a Norman-style youth club. You certainly won't find a gift shop, any loos, or statues of Mel Gibson like those that surround the William Wallace monument.

Everything of interest in south Devon is at the top of a hill, which means we all have sturdy calves and ruddy cheeks. The castle, however, is worth the walk. These days, Totnes is a transition town – one preparing for life after oil. Meetings are held in the church across the bridge discussing the re-skilling of the local community, which must learn to do without Morrisons, turn car parks back into market gardens, and learn to comb and spin greasy wool into garments in the event of global collapse. Totnes even has its own currency – the Totnes pound. The way the transition movement tells it, everyone will have a part to play when the oil wells run dry. The castle will form a splendid headquarters for transitioners, although it could probably do with a roof.

FOREVER TRANQUIL

Mary Smith
on Devon lanes

(*Daily Telegraph* 'Icons of England'
competition winner)

SHELTERED FROM THE BRIEF spring squall by the high banks on either side of me, I walk briskly to keep warm. Above me, clouds scud swiftly, framed by the bare branches of overhanging trees; seagulls, buffeted inland by the storm, slip sideways in the wind.

A gateway on my right draws me from the road. I lean on the top bar and survey the ploughed field. Newly turned soil lies glistening in long furrows – the rich red clay of south Devon.

This country lane was the scene of Sunday afternoon strolls during my childhood when, every week, we had to 'walk our Sunday lunch down'. Fifty years on, instead of my brother and parents I am accompanied by a walking stick. But the lane remains unchanged. Goose grass still grows along the hedgerow bottom, the same 'sticky willy' that I used to pick and plant on my brother's back.

The lane climbs gently upwards. The road has dried in the breeze, but the base of the bank is damp. It is always damp. It's where the ferns flourish and the grass is lush, where dog violets hide shyly in early spring and where frogs can be found.

The deep lanes of Devon remain untroubled by traffic. Fortunately drivers prefer the speedy routes via motorway or trunk road. Apart from the distant tractor sound, it's birdsong, not traffic noise, that keeps me company.

There are treasures in a Devon hedgerow. Obvious ones, like wildflowers, and hidden ones, like birds' nests in spring or a basking lizard in high summer.

I think of the flowers as stars. Vivid yellow stars are the first to appear – celandines, followed later by the pure white star-like stitchwort. The stars of summer are pink – roses, campion and herb robert, while autumn twinkles with bramble blossom. It shines out in palest pink and white amongst the tangle of other hedgerow plants.

In summer, the heady scent of honeysuckle adds even more enjoyment to a walk along a Devon lane, while autumn offers a harvest of hips, elderberries, sloes, nuts and blackberries.

I reach another gap in the bank. From the open gateway I have a view across rolling hills down to the Exe valley. The river is a silver ribbon; beside it parallel silver threads show the route of the railway that follows the river until it reaches the mainline station of Exeter St David's.

But Exeter is only a faint smudge in the far distance and here, in the beautiful Devon countryside, I am cocooned from its noise and pollution.

The lane continues to climb until it reaches Stoke Woods. These wooded heights are the site of a Roman signal tower and, earlier still, a fortified tribal encampment.

It's here that I stop and, like my forebears, I soak up the tranquillity of a Devon lane – the ultimate rural icon.

BRAVE NEW WORLD

Jon Snow
on Balcombe Viaduct

MY EARLIEST AND DEAREST horizon, it was the distant construct that defined where my world ended and the world beyond began. Yet it was no still or inanimate thing. Across it belched the steam of passing trains, together with the flickering lights of passenger traffic that promised destinations I had never seen or imagined.

For years, Balcombe Viaduct was beyond the point that either my large-wheeled perambulator or my small legs could ever reach. It was a journey of whose conquest my older brother would boast. But in my earliest memories I never got close enough for it to assume a scale much bigger than the one enjoyed from my bedroom window.

I grew up in the headmaster's house at Ardingly College, deep in the Sussex Weald. I shared a room until I was five or six, when I was finally allowed my own space. The nursery was divided in two and a window was cut in the wall that looked out on the viaduct. In the battle over rooms, I just knew I had to have the one with the viaduct.

In the foreground of my new and ever-present view lay my father and mother's labour of love – the garden. The lawn, the rock garden and the herbaceous border gave way to the orchard and Cox's orange pippins. The scent of the *Magnolia grandiflora* wafted up from the terrace. Beyond the garden, the lake and the nine-acre playing fields lay the bluebell woods and, finally, the viaduct. In high summer, the green of the fields was flanked by Farmer Woods' ripening corn, until the weeks in which I would watch his rickety reaper-binder laying stooks.

It wasn't until I turned nine or ten that I – with my two brothers – first walked all the way to the viaduct. Nearing it, its overwhelming scale filled us with fear. Towering a hundred feet above us, the oval openings in the brickwork of each arch were too high for us to clamber into. We counted the thirty-seven massive arches, and wondered how they could have been built as early as 1840 – with eleven million bricks. Every now and then the shattering clatter of a train above us would stir deeper fears. When all was quiet, however, we marvelled at the pinks and greys of what I now know to have been imported Dutch bricks – the creeping yellow splashes of lichen spread like liver spots.

We never saw a soul there. The viaduct was somehow our private pyramid, our eighth wonder of the world. Yet it was not its daunting, huge thousand metre width span that made it so special to me, or the number of trains that crossed it each day. It was its utter permanence at the rim of my world – somehow always there, the backdrop to my playing, my tricycling, my bicycling and my growing up. Somehow, I imagined that all children had a viaduct in their world.

It's still there now, restored, vast and busy. I cross it often en route to see my own child studying in Brighton, I have gazed from it, but not at it, for more than a quarter of a century. In many ways, I do not need to. It is where it belongs – on the edge of my innocence, before I deserted it and found out what lay beyond.

A SLOW BOAT TO BRISTOL

Kevin Spacey
on canal boating

HAVING LIVED IN LONDON for a number of years, I've started to make a real effort to explore a little more of England's great countryside. The sheer volume of attractions, often peculiar-looking monuments and dramatic landscape, makes any trip beyond the M25 sound pretty exhausting. But, I have to say, I'm never disappointed.

One of my favourite excursions last year was hiring a double-berth canal boat to cruise up and down the Kennet and Avon Canal – stopping off at every pub along the way. I know the English love to talk about the weather and it was amazing that weekend, with bright sunshine and little fluffy white clouds. It's a great way to watch the world drift by and it's a lot more relaxing – if a little faster perhaps – than travelling through London's streets. What better way is there to experience the spectacular Avoncliff Aqueduct and the nature that surrounds this man-made canal?

Of course, with every canal-boating holiday comes the obligatory pub stop at one of the many drinking establishments that line the Kennet's banks. And it was at the Cross Guns pub, next to a beautiful old and deserted mill, with a stream running past the end of the garden, that I developed a taste for cider. In America, we don't drink much of the stuff – or at least I don't – so it was a lot of fun to discover that for the first time. It was also where I discovered how hard it is to steer a canal boat after three or four pints.

Cider wasn't the only highlight. Forget restaurant dining, eating on the roof of the boat under the stars –

which are so much brighter than they are in London – is wonderful. And I would certainly recommend getting closer to – if not going in – the water. My friends had brought with them six inflatable dinghys from Asda. One afternoon we ended up floating down the river that runs alongside the canal with our arms and legs hanging over the edge – very *Swallows and Amazons*. The river was freezing, but when the sun is shining and the water is so clear you can almost see the bottom, nothing else really matters.

Remarkably, I managed to survive the weekend without falling into the canal. But sadly the same can't be said for my little dog, Mini. She got elbowed off the boat and, rather amusingly, a friend – who was on the roof when it happened – dived in to save her. By the time he came up for air, however, she was on the bank of the canal shaking the water off her hair. We laughed a lot, but as you can imagine, he didn't.

I did get spotted as we were going through Bradford-on-Avon and found ourselves in a rather menacing-looking lock. There were lots of people around drinking in the pubs, and when one of the locals asked if I was Kevin Spacey, my friend thought it would be funny to tell him I was Kevin's double, Geoff. This became a running joke for the rest of the weekend.

The thing I love about the countryside is that you never quite know what you're going to get. The weekend after drifting through the wonderful West Country, I was up to my knees in mud at the Glastonbury Festival. But then, I suppose that's what makes it such fun. This year, I intend to make it to the Lake District for a slightly less muddy and eventful trip – although I hear it does rain a lot up there. I have been told such wonderful stories about it, and a friend suggested I might be able to hire Wordsworth's old cottage if I ask the right people. But perhaps I should leave the dinghy at home this time!

THE WILD DIP

Rick Stein

on cold water swimming

RATHER LATE IN LIFE, I've discovered the pleasures of swimming in the cold sea around Padstow where I live. Walking early one winter morning round the Serpentine in Hyde Park two years ago, I saw a couple of wiry people coming out of a little hut wearing only swimming costumes, goggles and rubber caps, and heading straight for the water. In early summer, I joined their club. I was much taken by the advanced age of most of the swimmers, their good humour and rugged good health. I wanted to be like them. I haven't yet managed the complete initiation of swimming in the depths of January and February, the coldest months, but I do swim in the often chill, brown water out of season, sharing the lake with ducks, coots and Canada geese. Now, like my fellow members, I show an almost imperceptible surprise at those who choose to wear wetsuits

Soon after this, I started swimming around Padstow at Harlyn Bay and in the Camel Estuary, on which Padstow stands. At low tide the water in the estuary is reminiscent of the Serpentine, in the sense that I share it with many water-fowl, gulls and oystercatchers rather than ducks. And like the London pond it is shallow and has a muddy bottom. The smell is quite different, though, the dead shellfish and seaweed pong of estuarine mud not the best, but compensated for by the distant roar of the pounding on the Doom Bar near the mouth of the estuary. At high tide it comes into its own, and you swim with exhilaration in the swirling clean water, fighting against the strong ebb current which is trying to drag you down to Stepper Point. Eventually you give up, turn round and swim in an arc, hurtling down towards the mouth of the estuary, and then round to the pond–like calm of the water sheltered by a little peninsula of rocks.

At Harlyn Bay I wade out behind the surf and swim from one end of the beach to the other. It's always cold, even in the summer, but there is a delightful freshness about the seas around the British Isles.

Immersing oneself in cold water changes one's perception completely. One minute I can be preoccupied with worries, not least the absurdity of jumping into twelve degree water, and the next I'm only aware of the clouds, the cliffs, and the dark green trace of bladderwrack disturbed by my moving arms.

It is good in any season. This morning I watched a cormorant at high spring tide dive down to catch a sprat two yards away from me. The sun had just risen on a cold December morning so that all the windows in Padstow glinted. In summer, I love the early morning light before the sun has risen, the feel of the water; the fear of a wave breaking over you, the power of the white water tumbling you towards the beach or the fullness of the estuary at high tide, the smell of it. In April I pass people with my towel over my shoulder and they look at me as if I'm odd. After a swim at that time of year, almost delirious with the cold of it, I do feel odd, deliciously so.

THE LIGHT OF DAY

Roy Strong
on light and shade

FOR THOSE WHO LIVE in the country, the two most important days of the year are the winter and summer solstices. The summer one signals that the evenings will henceforth draw in – dusk falling progressively ever earlier until, by December, it can be pitch dark by five o'clock. And, a little before Christmas, comes the shortest day and the winter solstice – a signal that the days will begin to lighten and lengthen.

All of this passes virtually unnoticed in the city. Country living, however, exposes you to a whole range of natural light and shade effects of a kind unknown to urban man. The shift from getting up in the dark to arising in the light is a dramatic one. The night sky continues to be uniquely experienced in all its spangled glory. And to step out in summer and turn the eyes heavenwards is the source of an unforgettable delight.

Light conditions one's whole existence. It influences the orientation of a house – its aspect and which rooms are bathed in morning or evening light. How that light changes with the seasons and falls through the window of each room is a source of much fascination. The garden also springs to mind, for light affects where things are planted and whether or not they will thrive. Garden-making is an essay in design in terms of the manipulation of natural light, taking the visitor through contrasting effects, from gloom to dappled to the full glare of the sun.

Nature has a great way of using light and shade to turn a countryside scene into a work of art. These natural tools give the landscape its depth – establishing foreground and distance – and accentuate the geometry imposed by cultivation. And, because all of this is in a state of perpetual flux from one day to the next, the masterpiece is never the same. Rivers, streams and ponds are animated by the coming and going of light, making the water refract and sparkle or appear dense and mysterious. Each shaft of light catches a different detail; each dawn illuminates an otherwise hidden beauty.

For the vast majority of the population, light is and will always be something you get at the flick of a switch. It is there at the top of a lamp post, beaming away and dispelling any difference between night and day. The stars hardly exist in the city. But here in the country, I can still give thanks that light is what God intended it to be. Only in a landscape without artificial brightness does his great creative command: 'Let there be light' still hold true.

FORBIDDEN FRUITS

Alice Temperley
on cider farms

THEY ARE, FOR MANY, an integral part of our farming heritage. But our nation's cider farms and cider makers are not what they used to be. Growing up on a cider farm, we were taught from a young age to mourn the grubbing of an orchard. And I have done a lot of mourning since. In the past fifty years some fifty per cent of Somerset's orchards have now disappeared. And the once-familiar names of cider apples such as Brown snout, Chisel jersey and Kingston black sound ever more archaic.

It is perhaps because of their rapid demise that cider farms are now, for me, rather melancholic places. But it wasn't always that way. The autumns of my childhood were dominated by the hum of the apple press and the smell of fermenting apples. On frosty mornings I would accompany my father to help fork pomace (crushed apple remnants) to the orchard's sheep.

Each autumnal apple harvest brought with it a wonderful sense of community. I will always remember the motley crew of apple pressers that would arrive before the first light around harvest time. At dawn – on especially cold days – I was in charge of taking this weather-worn team fried breakfasts. I always enjoyed their bawdy camaraderie as they watched the sun rise over the mountains of apples piled in the yard.

In the orchard I was never alone. A notoriously fearsome pig called Ginger made a home among the apple trees. A bristling orange-and-black chicken-hunting monster, she was a worthy pig to taunt. She was, however, a force to be reckoned with, and her infamous jaws were avoided only by mad dashes around nearby tree trunks. When the pig alone didn't provide enough excitement, we would brave her in plastic cider barrels, which we would clamber into before rolling down the orchard.

Of course, we would inevitably hit a tree, scramble out, and embark on the life-and-death, tree-to-tree gauntlet before making it back to safe ground. Sadly, although the source of much enjoyment, Ginger the pig progressed from hunting and killing chickens to lambs and, after a stab at my mother's ankles, was banished to the freezer before she developed a taste for small children.

By preserving my memories, cider farms – with their vibrant apple trees – will remain the foundation from which I view the English countryside. They represent my childhood; I know and understand them. And, with any luck, they will continue to be an archetypal – albeit faded – vision of England in which I, too, can bring up my children.

POETRY IN MOTION

Nigel Thompson
on mist

A COUNTRYSIDE WITHOUT MIST is like a play without drama; a poem without emotion. Poet and author Edgar Allan Poe once said, 'Were I called on to define, very briefly, the term art, I should call it "the reproduction of what the senses perceive in nature through the veil of the mist".' I think he was right. As summer fades and the backdrop changes – swallows migrate from their telegraph wires and trees are drained of colour – it is the mist that clings to life and provides atmosphere. It is this shroud of liquid droplets suspended in the air that turns a rolling hillside scene into a work of art.

It is not so much the science of mist that fascinates me. It is the way it transforms a landscape as it descends. Mist is like a universal corrector in the way it veils the imperfections of the middle ground. It softens sharp edges and disguises the influence of man – it puts nature on show. I remember visiting the Lake District one October and seeing the mist linger over Grasmere. The hills stood tall above this blanket of air and the water crept out from beneath. It was like watching an artist put the finishing touches to an oil painting right before my eyes.

My life is one that has been spent close to water – I used to live in a water mill in the Lambourn Valley and now enjoy the view of a chalk stream near my home in Wiltshire – and it would be hard for me to imagine a world without mist. For twelve years I laboured over the vineyard on my land here in Stitchcombe, rising in the early autumn mornings to tend the vines and watch the grapes ripen. And it was on those mornings that I grew to love mist and all its mysteries. There is something about morning mist that is particularly compelling. I love watching it flow like a stream in the air; I love being enveloped in it along with thousands of dew-covered spider webs, protected from the weak shafts of light trying hard to make an impression on the scene. And I love breaking through it like the spires and tall trees on the horizon, and seeing it rest like a blanket of cotton wool before me.

Whether it is clinging to the contours of a hill or patching up a scene with its artistic strokes, the transient beauty of mist is something that has inspired generations of artists. With its unpredictable nature and dramatic undulations it brings romance and personality to the landscape, turning words on a page into an evocative scene. Keats' autumn was a 'season of mists and mellow fruitfulness'. For Wordsworth in 'Resolution and Independence', the mist took on a life of its own, chasing a hare in the glittering sun and running 'with her all the way, wherever she doth run'. With mist, characters from literature are lost, hidden and enveloped – but always remembered.

A countryside without mist is a countryside without art. Far from the glare of city lights and tightly packed buildings, mist will continue to spend autumn days perfecting its rural masterpiece – before the evening blanket descends to rub it all away.

THIS LAND OF DREAMING SPIRES

Simon Thurley

on spires

Boarding a train at London's King's Cross station and pounding up the East Coast Main Line, through York and Newcastle towards Edinburgh, is one of the great railway journeys of the world. Before your eyes – and from the comfort of your seat – passes some of our nation's greatest heritage. The cathedrals of Peterborough, York and Durham would make the line magical in themselves, but these are just three high points on a journey filled with historical delight and fascination.

I don't imagine many people notice the tall stone spire that lies eastwards across a water meadow just before the train races through Huntingdon. It belongs to St Mary's Church, Godmanchester, the parish church of the small town where I spent the first eighteen years of my life. How could the builders of that noble spire have guessed that half a millennium after it was completed, one of the town's sons would glimpse their work while travelling at the unimaginable speed of 125 miles per hour? How pleased would they have felt that their construction was still serving its original purpose?

Of course, we don't know the definitive reason why people started building spires on the towers of their churches. A spire certainly points upwards to God, so that may be the reason; but it is equally likely to have been driven by engineering. Medieval engineers were inventive and ambitious, and when it became possible to build something unusual and complicated, they did so with gusto. Above all, though, a spire must have been a marker – a way of identifying a place both geographically and economically.

Back on the East Coast Main Line, think of the spires of Newark and Grantham. They are small towns today, and it's nice to know where they are, but why such extraordinary spires? These were towns on the Great North Road, the artery linking London and Edinburgh. These prosperous little places were vying with each other for the trade of travellers. Their spires reached higher than those in neighbouring towns, like children in a classroom raising their hands higher in the hope the teacher will notice them first. These spires of England are the exclamation marks of our countryside, punctuation that not only tells you where you are, but helps you gauge the former economic condition and self-regard of a place.

Salisbury Cathedral now has the tallest spire in England (its great rival had been Old St Paul's in London, which lost its spire to a bolt of lightning during the reign of Queen Elizabeth I, and was then destroyed in the Great Fire of London of 1666). But what others lack in height, they make up for in number – Lichfield, for instance, with its three spires, is unique. But, for me, these competitions in spire envy are less interesting and beautiful than the village spires seen half-shrouded in mist, set against a sunset or behind a flock of emigrating swallows, or glimpsed rising above a leafy tree canopy or against a filigree of bare branches and twigs. Rarely in the history of architecture have man and nature conspired to produce so much beauty.

HEAVEN IN A WILD FLOWER

Alan Titchmarsh
on England's flora

THERE IS A DAY in late spring or early summer when, like Mole in *The Wind in the Willows*, I am forced out of the house by some deep-seated animal instinct. I can no longer sit at my desk attempting to weave a modest kind of magic with words. I must escape into the countryside and be a part of it.

I live in an old farmhouse surrounded by fields and woods, copses and hedgerows, meadows and hawthorn-canopied bridleways, so it takes only a few minutes before I am wading through wild flowers, listening to birdsong. I know some of the birds by name – quite a lot of them, I suppose – but I am especially familiar with the flowers. It is somehow more satisfying. Birds are busy, demanding to be noticed, capable of arousing curiosity in even the most indolent of passers-by. But flowers make no fuss, except in the exuberance of their blossom, and some of them do even that with commendable reserve. The moschatel, the symbol of Christian watchfulness, is barely three inches high with five lime-green flowers that look north, south, east, west and upwards in the direction of heaven; dog's mercury – hardly a flower at all, just a modest green tassel – indicates that a particular patch of woodland has been in existence since the Middle Ages. And by the river, the bashful, nodding water avens rests with its round-shouldered blooms of burnished copper that never dare to look you in the eye.

I love their names – lady's bedstraw and red campion, Queen Anne's lace and herb Paris – each one a link with countrymen of the past, who gave them their strange-sounding monikers. Schooled in botanical Latin, I know them also as *Paris quadrifolia* and *Arum maculatum*. But it is the mystery bound up in their common names that soothes me now.

I'll find a spot by the hedgebank that borders a field just above our house where I can sit in the warm, sweet cocksfoot grass and look down on the pantiled roof. I'll see the surface of our pond glinting, bright as a diamond in the morning sun. Swallows will skim it, skilfully slaking their thirst on the wing; the distant whistle of a steam train on the Watercress Line will take me back to my childhood in the Yorkshire Dales, where Mum and I went off in search of wild flowers.

I still have those wild flowers, pressed flat in a rough album – their names added in a spidery scrawl courtesy of nine-year-old fingers and a first Platinum fountain pen. Underneath the tissue paper removed from our daily loaf of bread, they are held fast in their desiccated glory – evergreen alkanet, fox and cubs, and wood sorrel – each one a memory of a moment in the summer of 1958 when they were plucked from Middleton Woods or the banks of the river Wharfe. Once home, they'd be sandwiched between the pages of the *Ilkley Gazette* before being slipped under the rag rug that ran from the kitchen to the living room, where the family feet could press them flat within a week.

It is fifty years now since the names of these flowers became as familiar to me as my own. They are a stirring reminder of a time when life was beginning to reveal its riches, its joys, its complexities and its heartbreaks. Crisp and lifeless they are now, and yet within them is captured a moment in childhood – an awakening to the wonders of nature. English wild flowers continue to captivate me more than any exotic species. They belong to my neck of the woods, my childhood, my life. Nodding in the hedgerow, blowing in the meadows and dipping their toes into the river, they enchanted a small boy to whom nature seemed more straightforward than people. In so many ways, it still does.

ALONE ON THE MOORS

Mark Tully
on moorland

CHESHIRE IS AN UNDERRATED county, often dismissed as nothing more than a posh dormitory for the two great cities of Manchester and Liverpool. But, as a child, it was home to me and my five siblings, after my parents brought us back from India, where we were born. And I came to love it dearly.

The countryside, with its lush green fields grazed by shorthorn cattle, its farmhouses and smart, manicured villages, is comforting and domesticated. Where we lived was also, like most of Cheshire, flat. So it's not surprising I was excited when we started the climb from the town of Macclesfield – once famous for its silk – up to the moors on the Cheshire–Derbyshire border to picnic.

The moors were wild, untamed and sparsely populated – the opposite of our home countryside. Instead of cows contentedly chewing grass, sheep nibbled coarse turf. Heather, a deep purple in season, covered much of the landscape, and weather-beaten grey stone walls, which seemed to have come from a different age, straggled across the hillsides. As we climbed up to the Cat and Fiddle – said to be the highest pub in England – we would often drive into a thin mist.

Wherever they are in England, moors still excite me. They have the primeval quality of mountains and the sea. In the same way, they convey a sense of the grandeur of nature, so much greater than anything we humans have created. The quality of the moors, however, which differentiates them from other places of breathtaking natural beauty, is their bleakness. It's a humbling bleakness, which often gives me a feeling of being small and insignificant.

Our moors are wild, empty places. Shakespeare's *King Lear* railed against 'filial ingratitude' on a wild heath, while Macbeth met the witches on a blasted one. It was the wildness of the Yorkshire moors that inspired Emily Brontë to create one of the most disturbed and disturbing characters of English literature, Heathcliff. And *The Hound of the Baskervilles* – the Sherlock Holmes adventure that terrified me when I read it as a child – is set on Dartmoor.

Looking out on the moors, I see a world without boundaries. Open like the sea, they seem to go on for ever. And in a small and crowded country like England, I find this openness particularly precious and awe-inspiring. It reminds me of Gerard Manley Hopkins' poem, 'The Grandeur of God'. For him, such grandeur was not frightening. He saw in it evidence that the 'Holy Ghost over the bent world broods with bright breast and ah! bright wings.' I and many others also find that the grandeur of God does, in Hopkins' words, 'flame out' in nature. It flames out in places where we humans have intervened least; places we have allowed to remain close to nature; places like the English moors. So long may they remain bleak, wild, empty and open.

TAKING FLIGHT

Charlie Waite
on wartime airfields

MY FATHER, REX WAITE, never told me very much about what he did in the war. Perhaps he knew that I would not take it in. He was middle-aged when I was born and so was a rather distant figure throughout my childhood, but one of whom I am immensely proud. The crowning achievement of his career was his brainchild, Berlin Airlift, a way of getting food and fuel to Western-occupied sectors of Berlin. An award for charity is given in his name at RAF Cranwell Training College each year – he was in the first intake in 1918. That's why, when I think of England's strengths as a nation, I think not only of its beautiful landscape, but also of its people and its history – my father and the airfields of Lincolnshire.

Travelling up to Lincolnshire on a blustery January day, it was impossible not to be struck by the light – a result of the flat fields and vast sky that made the county perfect for the many airfields built here in the lead-up to the Second World War. I found it quite hard to pin down an exact figure for the number operational in Lincolnshire throughout the war. But of those that were used, I believe only four remain. What seems obvious from this is not only how important Lincolnshire was in maintaining our defences, but also how the end of the war and the demands of modern warfare forced the county's landscape to adapt.

I was lucky enough to get fine weather on my visit. But as you drive on to the disused concrete runway at RAF Metheringham, it is not hard to imagine the thoughts of young pilots setting off on dangerous night missions to face enemy fighters and frostbite. This land was perfect for runways, but attracted fog. And for a pilot, exhausted and strained to breaking point, the appalling visibility must have required a superhuman effort.

Apart from the memorial to the Dam Busters at Woodhall Spa, I was surprised to find only a few reminders of the past. There are a small number of roadside plaques, names engraved on the flecked granite; there is an image of a Lancaster bomber painted on to a swinging village sign, and the walls of a pub covered entirely with photographs of smiling faces with their planes. And on a trip from airfield to airfield, it is just the odd spot of grass-fringed, fractured concrete that betrays signs of each one's turbulent history.

There seemed to be little left of my icon. But perhaps it is this physical lack of evidence that, in some paradoxical way, speaks volumes about Lincolnshire's recent past. The overgrown grass may disguise its scars, but the passing of some sixty-five years does little to drown out the voices of a thousand crews and the deep grumble of their bombers still hanging in the Lincolnshire air.

In fact, one visit to RAF Cranwell is enough for me to see that my icon is not just a patch of land carved out of the countryside. It is an icon of many faces. When I think of these disused airfields, I think of the young pilots who have passed, and continue to pass, through its doors. I think of the photograph of my father that hangs on the wall there – his face looking out from the 'Class of 1920'. I think of the Lancaster itself and the inventors, aviators and servicemen who have helped shape and defend this delightful country. Without such inspirational people, the countryside would be a lonely place.

THE DAWN CHORUS

Chris Watson
on birdsong

A JUMBLE OF WARBLED notes tumbling down through the bare branches of a large beech tree was the starting point for me this year. It was mid-January. A mistle thrush, head thrown back, was singing powerfully into the face of a cold wind from the highest point in the canopy. I was grateful to that bird. Not only did the song lift my spirits on an otherwise cold and grey day, but it also reminded me of what was to come. This single bird song, these solo notes, would develop into a chorus of bird songs, gradually stirring across the whole of England.

As the January daylight lengthened, other birds joined in. Robins began their evensong; a song thrush established a song post on a television aerial and broadcast its beautiful repertoire of repeated phrases. And from deep within the leafless twigs of our cotoneaster hedge, I heard the muted tones of blackbird subsong – a quiet and peculiar rehearsal for the full performance during the weeks to come. It's in the woodlands, however, where the volume of song builds most. Agile nuthatches pipe their sweet notes from high branches and on early mornings the still atmosphere vibrates with one of early spring's most exciting 'songs' – great spotted woodpeckers drumming, rattling a tattoo on a favourite tree.

These birds are our resident solo performers, advertising for a mate or establishing and defending a territory. During February we can isolate and localize these individuals as pinpoints of sound in the awakening woodland canopy. And then, one day in March, when the sound builds and the intensity increases, there is a change. I hear it twice or more before I actually stop and listen . . . Is it the end of a wren's song? An aberrant chaffinch phrase? No. It is the sound of the first willow warbler. Unseen but clearly heard – a silvery descending song from somewhere above. Within moments, my ears also pick up another recent migrant's tune – the jazz-like rhythm of the onomatopoeic chiffchaff. Over the next couple of weeks these warblers are joined by redstarts, pied flycatchers and secretive blackcaps. Eventually, the line-up is complete.

In late April, I always keep a weather eye open for a high-pressure system over Northumberland, and then make my move. I arrive on the edge of 'my' woodland in the middle of the night (around 2.30 a.m.) and cable a stereo microphone sixty metres away, underneath a small stand of oak trees. Perched on my camping stool, with headphones on, I listen and wait. At 3.12 a.m., a redstart sings and is quickly followed by a robin – with a territorial reply across the clearing – then song thrush, wren and blackbird.

The notes, phrases and songs mix and melt into a rich wall of sound, and this dawn chorus seems to light the spark for sunrise. At our latitudes I believe we have the very best dawn chorus in the world. Characterized by its slow development – a kind of evolution each new year – all the solo performances coalesce into a new sound and release an outpouring of song from our woodlands. It's our own private chorus that transforms the darkness into light.

BEAUTIFUL
EVENINGS

Francis Wheen
on village cricket

THERE ARE FEW LOVELIER words in the English language than 'bucolic', and few scenes evoke it as beguilingly as a village cricket ground. It is a late Sunday afternoon in rural Essex, in the first week of September. Sheep graze in an adjoining field, occasionally raising their woolly faces with a quizzical look at a roar of 'Howzat!' A late-summer breeze rustles the branches of oak trees which have been silent spectators at this pastoral performance for more than a century. Those drizzly grey clouds that seemed so menacing three hours ago have long since floated off in the direction of Chelmsford.

Eric, the bowler, celebrated his seventieth birthday last week, but his gentle off-breaks are almost as steady as when he first played for the village, a few years after the fall of the Attlee government. One of the batsmen at the crease is my stepson, a strapping teenager; the other is me. In the pavilion, a couple of girls scavenge for the remnants on the tea tables – a cheese-and-pickle sandwich, the last slice of chocolate cake. My young sons frolic just beyond the boundary with a tennis ball and a borrowed bat. The church bell tolls six o'clock; the vicar has arrived for evensong. Shadows lengthen.

Harold Pinter never wrote a more resonant line than that describing one of his bunk-offs from RADA to watch Middlesex at Lord's – 'that beautiful evening Compton made 70'. It's the word 'evening' that adds the magic. Think of any memorable cricket verse, such as Henry Newbolt's 'There's a breathless hush in the Close tonight/Ten to make and the match to win . . .' Or, better still, Francis Thompson's elegiac musings at Lord's:

For the field is full of shades as I near a shadowy coast,
And a ghostly batsman plays to the bowling of a ghost,
And I look through my tears on a soundless-clapping host
As the run-stealers flicker to and fro, to and fro . . .

Meaningless, I'd guess, to children who know only the modern urban game – the razzmatazz of Twenty20 matches played under floodlights in dayglo polyester tracksuits, with 'Another One Bites The Dust' blasting over the PA at the fall of each wicket. But they can still catch a glimpse of something more ancient and English and almost immutable if they happen to look out of a train window while rattling through the shires: something with the heady aroma of leather, mown grass, linseed oil and egg sandwiches. At twilight they may even notice the weary cricketers leaving the crease and adjourning to the pub across the road, the Leather Bottle.

Eric, having taken five wickets, is obliged to buy a jug of beer, shared with his teammates and opponents as they muse on another sublimely pointless day, and the end of another summer. No more slogs over square leg until next spring: sheep may safely graze. The half-dozen worshippers at evensong have gone home, shriven and blessed, to prepare for another working Monday, after a final chorus of 'Abide With Me'. Even so: if you return to the cricket ground as the darkness deepens and wander past the shuttered pavilion, you may discern that ghostly batsman playing to the bowling of a ghost, just as he did when old Eric was a boy. Other helpers fail and comforts flee; this abides.

ALFRED'S CAKES

Michael Wood
on historic Athelney

BORN IN AN INDUSTRIAL city in the cold north, it always seemed to me that the south-west was the real England. Somerset in particular – the 'summer land' as it was etymologized by medieval writers – for me was the mythic landscape of our history. On childhood trips there in my dad's old blue Austin 9, I used to think that if one stared hard enough, the past was still reachable – that you might still see its ghosts. And even these days, when I go down to visit my in-laws, between the reassuring surroundings of Bath's Roman springs and the soft contours of the Quantocks, I can't stop myself musing on the stories of English history. There's one place that stands for the whole tale of this island nation. It's an unprepossessing spot, easy to miss on the A361 from Glastonbury to Taunton. But, for me, it is the most resonant landscape in our nation's history: Athelney.

The story of Athelney takes us back to the Viking age, in the winter of 877–8. Alfred, the young king of Wessex – whom we know as the Great (he's the only person in our history to merit such a nickname) – is surprised and routed while celebrating Christmas at Chippenham. He takes refuge with a small warrior band in the Somerset marshes. The place was an inland sea in those days, a patchwork of islands and swamps, 'only reachable by punt' says Alfred's friend and biographer, the Welshman Asser. This 'Isle of Princes' was a place where the king must have hawked and hunted from boyhood, and it was there he hid while the Vikings harried Wessex. Homeless and with nothing to live on except what he and his band could forage for, his idea of

England – our England – hung by a thread; his kingdom shrunk to a few square miles of watery wilderness.

'Then after Easter,' says Asser (and you can almost sense the quickening of his pulse as he writes), 'he built a fort at a place called Athelney . . . from where, with the thegns of Somerset, he struck out tirelessly on raids against the Vikings.' Events then led to a surprise attack on the main Viking army in Wiltshire around 9 May (under the White Horse at Westbury). Following a savage clash of arms, the surge of shield walls and the rush of spears, Alfred wins and England is saved. The rest is history.

So Athelney was the key. To find it today, stop on the A361 at Lyng church, which still stands over a big defensive ditch of Alfred's time. At the end of the village you can walk on to the causeway, which Asser describes as leading across the swamp to the island where the fort was constructed. The island is now a low mound above the river Tone. To commemorate his victory, Alfred later built a little monastery here, which survived until Henry's Reformation, when the last monks were pensioned off and the buildings plundered for their stone. Nothing now remains above ground.

Even swiftly told, it's an epic tale. And, of course, legends soon gathered around it. Within a couple of generations, the story was told that in the marshes that spring, the starving Alfred had shared his last meagre rations with a wandering pilgrim. That evening his men came back, rejoicing in a miraculous catch of fish, and they all ate and slept well. And that night the pilgrim appeared to Alfred in a dream in his true form. He was none other than St Cuthbert, who prophesied for Alfred a kingdom of all England and for his descendants, rule over Britain (indeed, our present queen can claim Alfred among her ancestors).

The other tale of Athelney is the most famous of all legends about Alfred. The story goes that, while in the marshes, the desperate king sheltered incognito in a peasant's hut and was charged by the wife to watch the oven. He burnt her bread and was fiercely scolded. The Victorians loved the story, and you'll still find it in junk shops, referred to on cigarette cards and biscuit tins, and in old children's books and cartoons. (My favourite is from *Punch*, May 1941 – 'Well I suppose they are a *little* overdone,' says the king lugubriously, 'but what does that matter in wartime?')

Of course it sounds like a pure fairy tale, and scholars have dismissed it. But the story of the 'cakes' first appears in a text of the 970s or 980s, when there were people (like the Somerset man Archbishop Dunstan) who, in their youth, had talked to those who were there – one hundred years is not long at all in a memorizing society. I wonder then whether the scholars have been a little too stern in rejecting the story? Asser tells us that the king 'had nothing to live on'. Is it a coincidence then that two tenth-century stories about that fateful time both concern that essential of guerrilla war – food? Exaggerated it may have been in hindsight, as such things are, but it is not hard to imagine an old veteran of Athelney, sitting in retirement with his grandchildren in his orchard near Bath, forty years on: 'Food? Did you say food? Well now, here's a story. You'll never guess what happened to the king one day when we were in Athelney . . .'

MY ADVENTURE PLAYGROUND

Benjamin Zephaniah
on the Malvern Hills

FOR AN INNER-CITY kid who grew up in the 1960s, there was really only one place to go on holiday – Butlins. In fact, if you weren't holidaying at Butlins you weren't usually going anywhere at all. But as a city kid from a large family, the world of knobbly knees contests and Redcoats was always just beyond reach for me. And, looking back, it seems I had a lucky escape. For when your childhood holidays involve the back of a family camper van and the Malvern Hills, you are never far from adventure.

I will always remember the first time my dad parked up and let us run free on the hills. I felt like an animal set free from a leash. For me, it wasn't that the Malvern Hills was an Area of Outstanding Natural Beauty – I certainly wouldn't have known that it was designated as one the year after I was born in 1959. At that time, I didn't really notice the varying landscapes – the forts, rolling pastures, open commons and ancient woodland. This sea of green was my massive playground. In Birmingham, playing outside meant scrabbling over bomb sites, what we called bombpecks, and digging out old brooches and photos from the rubble. But here, in this vast space, I could play on land without fences, breathe in the clear air and run wild over the hills.

Of course, in my Malvern Hills, the hills were mountains; a den made of branches, my palace in the wild. This was a place where the nine of us could live out our adventures – not all of which were without danger. A game of hide and seek certainly takes on a life of its own when you have miles of hillside in which to disappear. And I do remember losing my brothers on more than a few occasions. My sister had a close encounter with what seemed like the edge of a cliff at the time, and it wasn't until we reached down to her with a tree branch, and told her not to look down, that she was lifted to safety. It sounds like something out of a cartoon now, but back then, it felt like we were risking our lives.

I am no longer that child waving excitedly from the back of our camper van. But I can still visualize the routes we took across the hills, and the places we parked. In fact, although when I went back recently it didn't feel as big or as dramatic – I seemed to notice the buildings of Malvern a lot more – I think it means more to me now. Having travelled to Jamaica to rediscover my roots, I realized that, for my parents, the Malverns was not just a place to let the children run wild. It was the nearest thing to a piece of home in England.

Coming from a family where my 105-year-old grandmother has never seen a city, I consider the countryside, and not the streets of Birmingham, my real home. So much so that I now live in Lincolnshire. There is beauty to be found in its flat farming land and among its wildlife – especially a rather friendly barn owl that once accompanied me down a lane. But Lincolnshire will never be the Malvern Hills – my little piece of Jamaica.

SUPPORT OUR CAMPAIGN

Shaun Spiers
Chief Executive, CPRE

Campaign to Protect
Rural England

BY INVITING PEOPLE TO nominate their own 'icons of England', we ran the risk of ending up with some rather obvious choices – Stonehenge, Hogwarts, the changing of the guard at Buckingham Palace. Instead we have a very idiosyncratic and personal collection, an illustration of G. M. Trevelyan's belief that places 'have an interest or a beauty of association, as well as an absolute or aesthetic beauty'.

And not just places. Floella Benjamin's love of the English weather (a brave choice) goes back to her memory of first arriving in the country as a child. Richard Benson's beautiful piece on 'rural sensuality' focuses on a single moment from his youth.

One of the pleasures of reading these essays has been to enter into an imaginary dialogue with their authors, pitching one's own experience against theirs.

Jon Snow writes movingly about the Balcombe Viaduct – significant not so much as a structure or view, but as the backdrop to his growing up. Clearly this has great personal significance for him. But *his* viaduct may summon memories of other viaducts or great industrial structures that enhance the landscape. In my case, it makes me think of the magnificent Welland Viaduct in Northamptonshire, and the few remaining huts lived in by the navvies who built it.

Fiona MacCarthy's essay on Kelmscott Manor conjured up all sorts of memories for me. I used to walk or cycle to the house from Filkins, the village my parents moved to when I was eighteen. At that time I knew Morris more for his revolutionary politics than for arts and crafts, but I found it impossible not to be touched by the high-class doggerel embroidered around his four-poster bed:

The wind's on the wold
And the night is a-cold,
And Thames runs chill
Twixt mead and hill,
But kind and dear
Is the old house here,
And my heart is warm
Midst winter's harm . . .

Sebastian Faulks's piece on pub signs also brought back memories. I had a tutor at university who used to speak contemptuously of Britain as a 'pub culture'. I told him I agreed, it was terrible, while privately thinking that he could do with an hour or two in a friendly pub. Faulks is right that 'deliberately silly' new pub names are regrettable. But old and silly names are, of course, entirely acceptable.

One of my favourites is the Five Alls, now the last pub in Filkins. The five 'alls' in question are, from memory; the lawyer who pleads for all, the parson who prays for all, the soldier who fights for all, the farmer who feeds all (or is it John Bull, paying for all?) and the Devil who takes all. How drab it is when quirky local pubs are taken over by chains and given the name and sign and decor of a hundred other pubs – or, worse still, suffer the fate of so many old interwar roadside inns and became a fast food 'restaurants'.

Local distinctiveness matters. Small things, seemingly insignificant patches of countryside can be 'iconic' to those who love them. So, for instance, Terence Blacker's Lonely Road, with its 'ordinary beauty' is clearly not in the running to become a World Heritage Site. Indeed, he recounts how the local authority has dismissed it as being of 'unexceptional' landscape quality. But it is much-loved and well worth protecting.

So it is with the 'icons' in this book and thousands more across England. The fact that we still have so much variety, beauty and history in such a small, densely populated and commercially minded country is a tribute not least to the work of CPRE and its members over the last eighty-four years.

This work is not about stopping the clock. We energetically and effectively oppose all unnecessary developments, but we also make constructive suggestions for accommodating necessary developments, not least more affordable rural homes. If proper care is taken, development can even enhance rural areas. We work to protect the beauty and character we have, but we want to pass on to future generations even more that is worth treasuring.

CPRE is optimistic about the future. We recently published a very positive vision for the countryside in 2026, our centenary year. But there is no disguising the seriousness of the threats facing the countryside. When we polled over a thousand people on their favourite 'icon of England', the result suggested that our ten most popular icons face the risk of serious erosion or even extinction.

Our national icons are symbols of resistance to the homogenization of our culture and landscape – much as the Green Man carvings in Norman churches described by Paul Kingsnorth may have been symbols of political resistance almost a thousand years ago.

Such things as local pubs, red phone boxes, hedgerows and drystone walls, village greens (ideally with cricket played on them), local varieties of food and village churches and churchyards may not be economically 'viable' or essential to our existence. No doubt they could be rationalized, modernized, made more efficient. But they are essential to our quality of life and our sense of identity. They are a large part of what makes England worth protecting. CPRE will carry on that work.

'There are particular places in England that come as close to perfection as you're ever likely to find on this planet. The English countryside is incredibly beautiful, dangerously finite and inexpressibly precious. We can secure a better future for the English countryside. We must. And we will.'

Bill Bryson
President, CPRE

CONTRIBUTORS

Kate Adie, OBE
became a household name for her
award-winning work as the BBC's
Chief News Correspondent. She
now presents *From Our Own
Correspondent* on BBC Radio 4,
and is the author of four books,
including her bestselling
autobiography, *The Kindness of
Strangers.*

George Alagiah, OBE
presents the *BBC News at Six*
and *World News Today*. He has
won several awards, including
Amnesty International's Best TV
Journalist. He is a governor of the
Royal Shakespeare Company
(RSC) and is an active supporter
of Human Rights Watch.

Peter Ashley
is a writer and photographer
who champions everything that
makes England such a unique
and interesting place to live. He
wrote *Unmitigated England* and
More From Unmitigated England,
and edited *Railway Rhymes.*

Clive Aslet
is Editor-at-Large of *Country
Life*. He writes for the *Daily
Telegraph*, the *Sunday Telegraph*
and the *Sunday Times*. His
latest book, *The English House*,
came out in autumn 2008.

Paul Atterbury
is a writer, lecturer and
broadcaster. His special
interests include art, design
and the history of canals and
railways. He has written or edited
over thirty books, and since 1990
has been one of the experts on
the BBC's *Antiques Roadshow*.

Dame Joan Bakewell
is a broadcaster and writer. She
began her TV career in the
1960s with BBC's *Late Night
Line-Up*. She now presents
Belief on BBC Radio 3 and
Inside the Ethics Committee on
BBC Radio 4. She is Chair of
The National Campaign
for the Arts and spokesman
for older people, appointed
by the Labour government.

**Dr Muhammad Abdul Bari,
MBE, FRSA**
has worked as a researcher,
teacher and SEN specialist in
London. He is a trustee
of the International Muslim
Charity (Muslim Aid), and has
been Secretary General of the
Muslim Council of Britain since
June 2006.

Simon Barnes
is the multi-award-winning
chief sportswriter at *The Times*

and also writes the paper's 'Wildlife Notebook'. He is the author of fifteen books, including *How to be a Bad Birdwatcher* and *How to be Wild*.

Laura Barton
is a feature writer for the *Guardian*. She lives in London.

Sister Wendy Beckett
was born in South Africa and became a nun in 1946 in the order of the Sisters of Notre Dame de Namur. She became a Consecrated Virgin in 1970 and leads a contemplative lifestyle. She became well known in the 1990s, presenting a series of acclaimed art history documentaries for the BBC.

Antony Beevor
is a writer and historian and a former officer with the 11th Hussars. He is the author of several bestselling books, including *Stalingrad* and *Berlin: The Downfall, 1945*, and is Visiting Professor at the School of History, Classics and Archaeology at Birkbeck, University of London.

David Bellamy, OBE, Hon FIs
is an itinerant botanist who makes his home in County Durham, flanked by some of Britain's best grouse moors. He will have dined this Christmas on sustainable grouse glazed with heather honey.

Floella Benjamin, OBE
is an actress, independent producer, writer and children's campaigner. She starred in the iconic *Playschool* and *Playaway* for many years. Her production company has made a wide range of award-winning programmes including *Coming to England*, adapted from her book, which won an RTS Award in 2004. Her most recent television programmes are *Mamma Mirabelle* and the *Sarah Jane Adventures*. She also appeared in the hit film *Run Fat Boy Run*. She was Chairman of BAFTA-Television and is now Chancellor of Exeter University and a Deputy Lieutenant of Greater London.

Richard Benson
is a journalist who was brought up on a farm in Yorkshire. Helping his family with the enforced sale of the farm inspired his bestselling memoir, *The Farm: The Story of One Family and the English Countryside*.

Scyld Berry
is the editor of *Wisden Cricketers' Almanack* and is the *Sunday Telegraph's* cricket correspondent.

Harold 'Dickie' Bird, MBE
is a retired international cricket umpire. He umpired in sixty-six Test matches and sixty-nine One Day Internationals, including three World Cup Finals. He retired in 1998, but came out of retirement in January 2007 to umpire the XXXX Gold Beach Cricket Tri-Nations series.

Terence Blacker
is a novelist, biographer and author of children's books which have been translated into eighteen different languages. His biography *You Cannot Live As I Have Lived and Not End Up Like This: The Thoroughly Disgraceful Life and Times of Willie Donaldson* won widespread critical acclaim and was BBC Radio 4's Book of the Week. He writes a twice-weekly opinion column for the *Independent*.

Raymond Blanc, OBE
is one of the finest chefs in the world. His Le Manoir Aux Quat' Saisons has held two Michelin stars for twenty-five years. He has written numerous bestsellers, including *A Taste of My Life* and *Foolproof French Cookery*. He is the star of the BBC's *The Restaurant* and his own series, *Kitchen Secrets*, which aired on BBC2 in February 2010.

Ronald Blythe
is a writer and critic from Suffolk. Much of his writing reflects his East Anglian background. He is the author of *The Age of Illusion, The View in Winter* and *Akenfield: Portrait of an English Village*, which became an instant classic.

Rosie Boycott
is a journalist and author. She has been Editor of the *Independent*, the *Daily Express* and *Sunday Express* and is a regular guest on BBC Radio 4's *Start the Week* and *Question Time*. Her latest book, *Spotted Pigs and Green Tomatoes*, was published in paperback in 2008. Rosie is the Chairman of the London Food Board and food advisor to the Mayor of London.

Derry Brabbs
celebrates England's architectural and cultural legacy through his photographs. He has previously worked on books with Alfred Wainwright and has recently completed *Roads to Santiago*. His website is www.derrybrabbs.com

Julia Bradbury
grew up in Sheffield and is the presenter of *Countryfile, Wainwright Walks* and *Coast to Coast*.

Melvyn Bragg
was writer, editor and presenter of *The South Bank Show* for London Weekend Television from 1978 to 2009 and has been

Controller of Arts at LWT since 1990 (Head of Arts 1982–90). He presented BBC Radio 4's *Start the Week* for ten years and is also a prolific novelist. He was made a Life Peer (Lord Bragg of Wigton) in 1998.

Jo Brand

is a stand-up comedian and has appeared on many comedy shows. She is also the co-author and star of *Getting On*, a sitcom set on a hospital's geriatric ward which was partly inspired by her earlier career as a psychiatric nurse. Her autobiography, *Look Back in Hunger*, was published in 2009.

Bill Bryson

came to England in 1973 on a backpacking expedition and decided to settle. He wrote for *The Times* and the *Independent*, and has written many travel books, including *The Lost Continent* and *Notes from a Small Island*. His latest book, *At Home: A Short History of Private Life*, is published in 2010. He is also President of CPRE.

Vincent Cable, MP

is the Member of Parliament for Twickenham. He has been the Liberal Democrats' main economic spokesman since 2003 and was the acting leader of the Liberal Democrats from 2006 to 2007.

Adrian Chiles

is a broadcaster and writer. He is best known for presenting *Match of the Day 2*, *The Apprentice: You're Fired* and *The One Show*.

Eric Clapton

is a singer, songwriter and guitarist. He has had a successful solo career, as well as with The Yardbirds, Cream, and Derek and the Dominoes. He is the only triple inductee into the Rock and Roll Hall of Fame and has won or shared eighteen Grammys.

Sue Clifford

was on the first board of Friends of the Earth whilst a lecturer in planning at University College London during the 1970s and 1980s. She is the founder director of Common Ground and her books include, with Angela King, *Holding Your Ground* and *England in Particular: A Celebration of the Commonplace, the Local, the Vernicular and the Distinctive*.

Wendy Cope

was a teacher for nearly twenty years and went freelance shortly after the publication of her first book of poems, *Making Cocoa for Kingsley Amis* in 1986. *Two Cures for Love*, a selection of her poems, was published in 2008.

Nicholas Crane's
books include *Clear Waters Rising: A Mountain Walk Across Europe* and *Mercator: The Man Who Mapped the Planet*. He is presenter of the recent BBC series, *Coast*, *Map Man* and *Great British Journeys*. Nick is a Vice-President of CPRE.

Dan Cruickshank
is a regular presenter on the BBC, best known for his popular series, *Britain's Best Buildings* and *Around the World in 80 Treasures*. He is an Honorary Fellow of RIBA, a leading expert on architecture and historic buildings, and a frequent contributor to *The Architects' Journal* and *The Architectural Review*.

General Sir Richard Dannatt, GCB, CBE, MC
was commissioned into the Green Howards in 1971. He has served seven tours of duty in Northern Ireland, with the UN in Cyprus, two tours in Bosnia, and in Kosovo. He was Chief of the general staff from 2006 to 2009 and is currently Constable of the Tower of London.

Jonathan Dimbleby
is a writer, broadcaster and film-maker. He has presented *Any Questions?* and *Any Answers?* for BBC Radio 4 since 1987. In

2008 his five part series *Russia – A Journey with Jonathan Dimbleby* was broadcast by BBC2 and his latest book *Russia – A Journey to the Heart of a Land and its People,* was published to accompany the series. He is currently working on a BBC2 series about Africa. In addition to his Presidency of VSO, he is Chair of Index on Censorship and a Trustee of Dimbleby Cancer Care.

Wilfred Emmanuel-Jones
is a British businessman, farmer, founder of The Black Farmer range of food products, and also founder of a scholarship to encourage ethnic minorities to work in the rural community. He has been selected by the Conservative Party as their prospective parliamentary candidate for Chippenham in the 2010 general election.

Sebastian Faulks, CBE
is the author of eleven books, including *Human Traces, Charlotte Gray* and *Engleby*. He has been literary editor of the *Independent*, columnist for the *Guardian* and the *Evening Standard,* and is a Fellow of the Royal Society of Literature.

Bryan Ferry
is a singer and songwriter who came into prominence in the

1970s as the founder and lead vocalist of Roxy Music. He has since had a successful solo career, with eight UK top ten solo albums.

Dick Francis, CBE
was an author and retired jockey. Following his first book, the autobiography *The Sport of Queens*, he secured a sixteen-year position as Racing Correspondent at the *Sunday Express*. He had forty-three bestselling novels, starting with *Dead Cert* in 1962. He died in February 2010.

Trisha Goddard
was a TV reporter and presenter in Australia before coming to the UK. She hosted the popular daily talk show, *Trisha*, from 1998 to 2009 and is a patron of the mental health charity Mind. She lives in Norfolk.

Zac Goldsmith
is currently chairman of the *Ecologist* magazine and Deputy Chairman of the Conservative Quality of Life Policy Group. He has been selected by the Conservative Party as their prospective parliamentary candidate for Richmond Park in the 2010 general election.

Andy Goldsworthy
is an artist known for his outdoor sculptures and large-scale installations, such as 'The Sheepfolds Project' in Cumbria. His 2007 exhibition at the Yorkshire Sculpture Park was awarded the Southbank Award for Visual Arts.

Henrietta Green
is a food writer, broadcaster and founder of *www.FoodLoversBritain.com*. She is widely acknowledged as the country's leading expert on local and regional speciality food producers and is author of the acclaimed *Food Lovers' Guide to Britain*. To find out more about British cherries visit CherryAid at *www.FoodLoversBritain.com*.

Graham Harvey
is Agricultural Story Editor on *The Archers* and author of a number of books on food and the countryside. He wrote *The Killing of the Countryside*, which won the BP Natural World Book Prize. His latest book is *We Want Real Food*.

Tom Heap
is a presenter. He is currently kept busy with *Costing the Earth* on BBC Radio 4, alongside *Countryfile*, *Panorama* and *Animal 24:7* on TV. He worked at BBC news for thirteen years, latterly as Rural Affairs Correspondent.

Paul Heiney
is a writer and broadcaster, formerly a presenter of *That's Life* and *Watchdog*, he now presents *Countrywise*. He has also been an organic farmer since 1990. This experience inspired not only his hugely successful column, *Farmer's Diary*, which appeared weekly in *The Times* for seven years, but also a number of books.

Leo Hickman
is an environmental journalist and editor at the *Guardian* and writes a weekly column on ethical living. He is the author of several books, including: *A Life Stripped Bare: My Year Trying to Live Ethically*, *The Final Call: In Search of the True Cost of Our Holidays* and *Will Jellyfish Rule the World?*, a children's book about climate change.

Simon Hoggart
is a journalist and broadcaster. He writes on politics for the *Guardian*, and on wine for *The Spectator*. Until 2006, he presented *The News Quiz* on Radio 4. His journalist sketches have been published in a series of books.

Charlotte Hollins
manages Fordhall Community Land Initiative at Fordhall Organic Farm. She saved the farm from developers in 2006

and it is now Britain's first community-owned farm.

Elizabeth Jane Howard, CBE
has written several novels, television plays and a collection of short stories. Her first novel, *The Beautiful Visit*, won the John Llewellyn Rhys Prize in 1951. Others include *The Long View* and *The Cazalet Chronicles*, which were dramatized on BBC1. Her latest novel is *Love All*.

Margaret Howell
was born in Surrey and has always loved the English countryside. A designer of contemporary clothes, she is inspired by natural fabrics and traditional British craftsmanship.

Tristram Hunt
is a lecturer in British History at Queen Mary, University of London, and a Fellow of the Royal Historical Society. He is also the author, most recently, of *The Frock-coated Communist: The Revolutionary Life of Friedrich Engels*.

Maxwell Hutchinson
was President of the Royal Institute of British Architects from 1989 to 1991. He is a practising architect and

contributor to BBC Radio 4 and BBC2's *Newsnight*. He presented Channel 4's *Demolition Detectives*, wrote and presented *Number 57* and *The History of a House*, and worked on *First Sight* and *Restoration Nation*.

Kurt Jackson

is one of Britain's leading artists. He embraces different materials and techniques. An understanding of natural history and ecology, politics and the environment is intrinsic to his art.

Simon Jenkins

writes for the *Guardian* and the *Evening Standard* and chairs the National Trust. His books include *England's Thousand Best Churches, England's Thousand Best Houses* and most recently, *Wales: Churches, Houses, Castles*.

Terry Jones

is best known for being a member of Monty Python, but is also a screenwriter and director. His directorial credits include *Monty Python and the Holy Grail, Life of Brian, Monty Python's the Meaning of Life, Personal Services* and *Erik the Viking*. He is also the author of several children's books, including *Nicobobinus* and *Fantastic Stories*.

Paul Kingsnorth

is a writer and an environmentalist. He was previously deputy editor of the *Ecologist* and is the author of two books, *One No, Many Yeses* and *Real England*. In 2009 he co-founded the Dark Mountain Project, a new cultural movement for an age of global disruption.

Miles Kington

was a writer for *Punch* who wrote humorous columns in *The Times* and the *Independent*. He was often on BBC radio and was the author of the popular series of books, *Let's Parler Franglais!* He died in January 2008.

Satish Kumar

has been the editor of *Resurgence* for thirty-seven years. He is also Visiting Fellow at Schumacher College. He has written many books, including his autobiography, *No Destination*.

David Lodge

is a novelist, critic and Professor Emeritus of English Literature at the University of Birmingham. His latest novel is *Deaf Sentence*. Other works include *Author, Author!* and *Thinks*.

Gabby Logan
is a television and radio
presenter, as well as a former
international gymnast. She
currently hosts programmes for
BBC Sport, mainly focusing
on football, and a Sunday
morning radio show on BBC
Radio 5 Live.

Richard Mabey
is the author of some thirty
books of literary non-fiction,
including *Gilbert White*, which
won the Whitbread Biography
Award. He is Vice-President of
the Open Spaces Society and
patron of the John Clare Society.

Fiona MacCarthy, OBE
is a cultural historian best known
for her studies of nineteenth and
twentieth century arts, crafts
and design. Her biography of
William Morris won the 1994
Wolfson History Prize. She is a
Fellow of the Royal Society of
Literature, a Senior Fellow of
the Royal College of Arts and
was awarded the Bicentenary
Medal of the Royal Society
of Arts for services to art and
design.

Robert Macfarlane
is a travel writer and literary
critic. His first book, *Mountains
of the Mind*, won the *Guardian*
First Book Award and the
Somerset Maugham Award. His

second, *The Wild Places*, also
won a number of prizes and has
recently been adapted into a
one-hour film by the BBC.
He is a Fellow of Emmanuel
College, Cambridge.

Andrew Marr
is a writer and broadcaster.
He is the of host of *The Andrew
Marr Show* on BBC 1 and also
presents BBC Radio 4's *Start
the Week* every Monday
morning. He has also presented
*Andrew Marr's History of
Modern Britain* and *Andrew
Marr's the Making of Modern
Britain*.

Peter Marren
writes about wildlife, the
countryside and history.
His books include *The New
Naturalists* and *Twitching
Through the Swamp*. He has also
worked with Richard Mabey
on *Bugs Britannica*, which will
be published in May 2010.

Simon Sebag Montefiore
is a prize-winning historian:
his books include *Catherine
the Great & Potemkin*, *Young
Stalin* and *Stalin: Court of the
Red Tsar*. He is a Fellow of the
Royal Society of Literature.

Brian Moore
is a former rugby union player.
He played in three rugby World

Cups and was a member of the England side which won three Grand Slams. In 1991, he was voted Rugby World Player of the Year. He currently writes on rugby for the *Daily Telegraph* and is well known as a sports pundit for the BBC.

Dr Richard Muir
is the author of many books and articles on the history of the countryside, and has written a number of articles about landscape. He is an Honorary Research Fellow in Geography and Environment at Aberdeen University.

Daljit Nagra
is a poet. He currently lives and works in London as a secondary school English teacher. His first collection, *Look We Have Coming to Dover!* won the 2007 Forward Prize for Best First Collection and *The South Bank Show* Decibel Award in 2008.

John Julius Norwich
is a writer and historian and the author of *The Architecture of Southern England*. He has been General Editor of *Great Architecture of the World, The New Shell Guides to Great Britain* and *The Oxford Illustrated Encyclopaedia of Art*. He has also written and

presented several historical documentary films and is former chairman of the Venice in Peril Fund and of the World Monuments Fund.

Sean O'Brien
is a poet, critic, playwright and Professor of Creative Writing at Newcastle University. He received the Northern Rock Foundation Writer's Award in 2007. Much of his work has won awards, but most recently *The Drowned Book* was awarded both the Forward and T.S. Eliot Prizes. His first novel, *Afterlife*, was published in 2009.

Michael Palin, CBE
starred in the Monty Python sketches and films, as well as other TV series and films, including *A Fish Called Wanda*, which won him a BAFTA. He has also presented seven BBC travel documentary series. He is currently president of the Royal Geographical Society.

Jonathon Porritt, CBE
is an environmentalist and Founder Director of the sustainable development charity, Forum for the Future, Chairman of the UK Sustainable Development Commission and author of *Capitalism: As If The World Matters*.

Gavin Pretor-Pinney
is founder of The Cloud
Appreciation Society and
co-founder of *The Idler*
magazine. He wrote the
international bestseller, *The
Cloudspotter's Guide*. His next
book is called *The Wavewatcher's
Companion*.

Libby Purves, OBE
is a radio presenter, journalist
and author. She currently
presents *Midweek* on BBC
Radio 4 and the education
programme *The Learning Curve*.
She also writes a column for
The Times and is a regular
contributor to the *Oldie*
magazine.

Tony Robinson
presents the Channel 4 series
Time Team. As an actor he
has appeared in several series,
including *Blackadder*. He has
written numerous books and
won many awards from the RTS
and BAFTA for his TV writing.
He is president of the Young
Archaeology Club.

Alexei Sayle
is a writer and performer, he has
written several bestselling short
story collections and novels
including *Barcelona Plates*
and *Mister Roberts*. In 2008
he presented *Alexei Sayle's
Liverpool* for the BBC. He also

co-wrote and starred in *Alexei
Sayle's Stuff, The All-New Alexei
Sayle Show* and *Merrygoround* as
well as appearing in many films
and radio programmes.

John Sergeant
is a broadcaster, journalist and
writer, who has been chief
political correspondent at the
BBC and political editor of ITN.
He has written two bestsellers,
one of which is his memoir, *Give
Me Ten Seconds*.

Sir Antony Sher
is an acclaimed stage and film
actor and also a writer, theatre
director and painter.

Lucy Siegle
is a journalist, author and
presenter who specializes in
ecological and ethical lifestyle
matters. She contributes to the
Guardian and the *Observer*, and
magazines such as *Marie Claire*.
She is the author of *Green
Living in the Urban Jungle*.

Mary Smith
now lives in Bedfordshire, she
was born and spent most of
her childhood in South Devon.
She was formerly Head of the
French Department in a local
Middle School but has now
retired and can spend more
time on her first love, writing.
Her contribution to this book

was the winner of the *Daily Telegraph*'s 'Icons of England' competition.

Jon Snow
has been with ITN since 1976 and has anchored *Channel 4 News* since 1989. He has won a BAFTA and been RTS Journalist of the Year twice, and he has been a trustee of the Tate and National Gallery.

Kevin Spacey
is an Academy Award-winning American film and stage actor and director. His role in *The Usual Suspects* won him his first Oscar in 1996 and in 2000 he won Best Actor for *American Beauty*. Since 2003 he has been Artistic Director of London's Old Vic theatre.

Rick Stein, OBE
owns four restaurants in Padstow, Cornwall and is the author of eleven cookery books, including *English Seafood Cookery*. He has presented a number of cookery series for the BBC, including *Rick Stein's Taste of the Sea* and *French Odyssey*.

Sir Roy Strong
is a writer, art historian, lecturer, critic, columnist and regular contributor to both radio and television. He has been Director of both the National Portrait Gallery and the Victoria and Albert Museum. With his late wife he designed one of England's largest post-war formal gardens, The Laskett.

Alice Temperley
launched Temperley London in 2000. It has quickly grown to become one of the most desirable fashion brands in the world. She has won awards from *Glamour* and *Elle*, the Walpole Award for British Design Excellence, and has been named one of Britain's top thirty businesswomen.

Sir Nigel Thompson, KCMG, CBE
was chairman of CPRE from 2003 to 2008. He trained as a civil and structural engineer and spent his career at Ove Arup Partners, working with architects designing buildings.

Dr Simon Thurley
is a leading architectural historian and Chief Executive of English Heritage. He has been Director of the Museum of London, and Curator of Historic Royal Palaces. He has written several books and is a regular broadcaster, presenting programmes such as *Houses of Power*.

Alan Titchmarsh
is a gardener, author and broadcaster. He has written over forty books and novels, and now has his own daytime ITV show, featuring conversation, music and the arts. He also presents a BBC Radio 2 music programme on Sunday evenings.

Sir Mark Tully
was born in Calcutta and now splits his time between England and India. He was Chief of the Bureau for BBC New Delhi for twenty-two years and has written books such as *No Full Stops in India*, *The Heart of India* and *India's Unending Journey*.

Charlie Waite
is a landscape photographer who has published around thirty books and held exhibitions across Europe, the USA, Japan and Australia. His company, Light & Land, runs tours, courses and workshops worldwide. His website is www.charliewaite.com.

Chris Watson
is a sound recordist who specializes in wildlife sounds from around the world. He has released solo CDs and worked across film, television and radio. He won a BAFTA award for Best Factual Recording on the BBC's *Life of Birds*.

Francis Wheen
is a journalist, writer and broadcaster. He is the author of several books, including a biography of Karl Marx, which won the Isaac Deutscher prize. He is the Deputy Editor of *Private Eye*.

Michael Wood
is a historian, writer and broadcaster. He is the author of several highly praised books on English history, including *In Search of the Dark Ages*, *Domesday Quest* and *In Search of Shakespeare*. He has over eighty documentary films to his name, among them *In the Footsteps of Alexander the Great* and *The Story of India*. He is currently working on an English history series for the BBC.

Benjamin Zephaniah
is a writer, poet and musician. He writes poetry that is musical and political, gaining much of his reputation through performance. He has published novels for teenagers, as well as plays, and released numerous records.

ILLUSTRATION CREDITS

BAL= Bridgeman Art Library;
MEPL = Mary Evans Picture Library

15: Palace Pier, Brighton, photo by Tony Ray Jones, c. 1966: National Media Museum/SSPL; 18: 'View from Avebury steeple of Silbury Hill', engraving from *Stonehenge: a Temple Restored to the British Druids* by William Stukeley, 1740: Private Collection/BAL; 31: assortment of standard letter boxes, c.1935: British Postal Museum and Archive/ © Royal Mail Group Ltd/BAL; 35: *Ancient Trees, Lullingstone Park*, pencil drawing by Samuel Palmer, 1828: Yale Center for British Art, Gift of Paul Mellon/BAL; 39: Killin station, Perthshire, 1950s: Milepost 92 1/2 – railphotolibrary.com; 42: *Southend*, poster by Harold L. Oakley, 1941: © TfL from the London Transport Museum collection; 45: 'The Haunt of the Gulls', engraved illustration from *Leisure Hour*, 1888: Private Collection/BAL; 48: *A Hare Running, With Ears Pricked*, pen & ink drawing by James Seymour (1702-52): Yale Center for British Art, Paul Mellon Collection/BAL; 54: *A Lych Gate*, pencil drawing by John Sell Cotman, early 19th century: © Trustees of the British Museum; 57: *Military Orchid*, book-plate, 1869: MEPL; 65: '*England, with all thy faults, I love thee still (Cowper)*', cartoon by Carl Giles: © Express Syndication; 69: Castle Combe, Wiltshire: Charles Hewitt/Getty Images; 76: 'Scarborough Braces You Up – The Air Does It', NER poster, 1900-1922: NRM – Pictorial Collection; 84: plan of a garden, including an orchard, from *The New Orchard Garden* by William Lawson, 1618; 88: *Hart's Tongue Ferns*, wood engraving by Reynolds Stone, 1971: © Estate of Reynolds Stone; 92: *Trilobite from Golden Grove, 6th November 1841*, watercolour by John Phillips: © Oxford University Museum of Natural History/BAL; 96: Hadrian's Wall: © Derry Brabbs; 100: 'Rutlandshire with Oukham and Stanford', from *Theatre of the Empire of Great Britain* by John Speed, 1611-12: Private Collection/BAL; 103: Skiddaw: © Derry Brabbs; 109: a tug-of-war at the Tintern fete, South Wales: © David Hurn/Magnum Photos; 112: *A Windy Day on the Beacon*, 1855: MEPL; 115: leaflet for Motor Coach Tours circa 1950: Amoret Tanner/Alamy; 119:

limestone plateau, Malham Cove, Yorkshire, 1969: Edwin Smith/
RIBA Library Photographs Collection; 123: view of Eton College
over the Thames: 2d Alan King/Alamy; 126: *The Broads*, poster by
Anton Abraham von Anrooy, 1928: © Swim Ink 2, LLC/Corbis;
130: artist's reconstruction of the Euston Arch: Joe Robson/AVR
London; 136: *Common Thick-Knee*: 19th era 2/Alamy; 145: inn
sign from *The English Inn Past and Present* by A. E. Richardson
and H. Donaldson Eberlein, 1925; 149: Penshaw Monument,
Sunderland: © Aidan O'Rourke; 151: racehorses on the Ridgeway
near Lambourn, c.1955: John Gay/English Heritage NMR/MEPL;
154: Little Red Riding Hood puzzle page: Private Collection/©
Look and Learn/BAL; 162: Sheepfold MI87, Tilberthwaite Glen,
Cumbria rebuilt by Andy Goldsworthy: NVM Digital; 168: 'The
Sheep of his Pasture' by Edward Calvert, c.1828, from an edition
of 350 prints published for the album 'A Memoir' by Calvert's son:
Private Collection/BAL; 181: Westonbirt House, Gloucestershire,
1879: MEPL; 192: breakwaters, East Anglia: courtesy Margaret
Howell; 195: cliffs at Ilfracombe, Devon: 2d Alan King/Alamy;
198: 'A section through the roadway of Holborn Viaduct, London:
looking east, showing the middle level sewer', wood-engraving after
W. Haywood, 1854: Wellcome Library, London; 205: Hunsdon
House, anonymous 16th-century lithograph: Private Collection/
BAL; 208: view of Hampstead Heath, 1840: Alan King engraving/
Alamy; 212: Green Man, woodcut, c. 1630: MEPL; 219: 'Wistman's
Wood' drawn by Alfred Dawson from a sketch by J. L. W. Page,
from *An Exploration of Dartmoor . . .* by John Lloyd Warden Page,
1889; 222: 'The High Style' from Perils of Crinolines, 1859:
MEPL; 234: 'The East Front of Kelmscott Manor', frontispiece
of *News from Nowhere* by William Morris, woodcut by Charles
March Gere, 1892: Private Collection/BAL; 238: *The Old
Yarmouth Road at Blofeld* by John Sell Cotman (1782-1842), chalk
drawing: © Trustees of the British Museum; 242: newly-ploughed
field, Holkham, 1970: Edwin Smith/RIBA Library Photographs
Collection; 246: white horse, Uffington, Berkshire, 1949: Fred
Ramage/Keystone Features/Getty Images; 254: five-a-side football
coaching, 1980, photograph by Henry Grant: Museum of London;
258: woodcut illustration by Gwen Raverat to *Mountains and*

Molehills by Frances Cornford, 1934: © Estate of Gwen Raverat.
All rights reserved, DACS 2010; 264: front cover of 'John Bull',
June 1950: Private Collection/© The Advertising Archives/BAL;
268: Spurn point, Yorkshire: David Baker/Alamy; 271: Middleton
Dale, Derbyshire, 19th-century engraving: 19th era/Alamy; 275:
single tree in a field by John Cooper:Private Collection/© Special
Photographers Archive/BAL; 281: 'Cornwall', GWR poster, 1923-
1947: NRM – Pictorial Collection; 284: drawing of Mick Aston:
© Ruth Murray; 290: Great Tew, Oxfordshire, 1938: MEPL; 296:
Totnes Castle, Devon: © Andrew Payne/Alamy; 302: Balcombe
Viaduct, illustration by Curtis Tappeneden to *An Eccentric Tour
of Sussex* by Peter Bridgewater, 2007, Snake River Press; 305:
Canal Inn by George Mackley, 1969, wood engraving: © Bolton
Museum and Art Gallery/BAL; 309: Serpentine Swimming Club:
Peter Macdiarmid/Getty Images Europe; 315: girl sitting in an
orchard, photo by John Gay: © English Heritage/NMR; 318:
Brighton beach, Sussex, photo by Edwin Smith, 1950s: Edwin
Smith/RIBA Library Photographs Collection; 321: *Salisbury
Cathedral from the North West*, pencil drawing by John Constable,
1829: Fitzwilliam Museum, University of Cambridge/BAL; 324:
Red Rose Campion from Gerard's *Herbal*, 1597; 328: Bodmin
Moor, Cornwall: © The Marsden Archive; 331: Lancaster bomber,
Lincolnshire Aviation Heritage Centre, East Kirby: photo Charlie
Waite; 337: 'The Cricket Match', illustration by Robert W. Buss
to *The Pickwick Papers* by Charles Dickens, first published 1836;
340: Alfred the Great, engraving after William Small (1843-1931) :
Private Collection/BAL; 344: detail of a map of the west country
by William Hole from *Poluolbion* by William Drayton, 1616.

CAN YOU HELP US?

Campaign to Protect
Rural England

Formed in 1926, CPRE is one of the longest established and most respected environmental charities in England. CPRE is a network of over two hundred district groups; there's a branch of CPRE in every county, a group in every region, as well as a national office in London. We have over sixty thousand members and supporters.

CPRE's aim is for a beautiful and living countryside and we campaign nationally and locally for positive solutions for the long-term future of the countryside. By supporting CPRE, you contribute to the continued existence of a beautiful, tranquil and diverse countryside for everyone to enjoy. We hope that after reading this book you feel inspired to join our campaign. You can join us by:

- making a donation, regular gift or becoming a member of CPRE. Members receive our regular newsletter and discounted entry to over two hundred beautiful, historic and stately houses and gardens across England.

- volunteering with your local CPRE branch.

- becoming a guardian of our countryside by leaving a legacy in your will.

Find out more about us by visiting our website at **www.cpre.org.uk**, calling us on 020 7981 2800, contacting us at **info@cpre.org.uk** or writing to CPRE, 128 Southwark Street, London, SE1 0SW.

Registered charity no: 1089685